First World War
and Army of Occupation
War Diary
France, Belgium and Germany

12 DIVISION
Divisional Troops
69 Field Company Royal Engineers
and 70 Field Company Royal Engineers
31 May 1915 - 10 May 1919

WO95/1840

The Naval & Military Press Ltd
www.nmarchive.com
Published in association with The National Archives

Published by

The Naval & Military Press Ltd

Unit 10 Ridgewood Industrial Park,

Uckfield, East Sussex,

TN22 5QE England

Tel: +44 (0) 1825 749494

www.naval-military-press.com

www.nmarchive.com

This diary has been reprinted in facsimile from the original. Any imperfections are inevitably reproduced and the quality may fall short of modern type and cartographic standards.

© **Crown Copyright**
Images reproduced by permission of The National Archives, London, England, 2015.

Contents

Document type	Place/Title	Date From	Date To
Heading	1840/1 69th Field Coy R.E.		
Heading	12th Division 69th Field Coy. R.E. May 1915-May 1919		
Heading	12th Division 69th F.C.R.E. Vol I June Jly Aug to Sept 15		
War Diary	Aldershot Southampton	31/05/1915	31/05/1915
War Diary	Harve	01/06/1915	02/06/1915
War Diary	St Omer	03/06/1915	03/06/1915
War Diary	Wins	04/06/1915	05/06/1915
War Diary	Cinq-Rues	06/06/1915	06/06/1915
War Diary	Noot Boom	07/06/1915	07/06/1915
War Diary	Erquinghem	08/06/1915	15/06/1915
War Diary	Le Verrier	16/06/1915	19/06/1915
War Diary	Erquinghem	20/06/1915	20/06/1915
War Diary	Ploegsteert	20/06/1915	08/07/1915
War Diary	Armentieres	09/07/1915	30/09/1915
Heading	12th Division 69th F.C.R.E. Vol.2 Oct 15		
War Diary	Vermelles	01/10/1915	12/10/1915
War Diary	East of Vermelles.	13/10/1915	19/10/1915
War Diary	Vandricourt	20/10/1915	25/10/1915
War Diary	Annequin	26/10/1915	31/10/1915
Heading	12th Division 69th F.C.R.E. Vol. 3 Nov 15		
War Diary	Annequin	01/11/1915	24/11/1915
War Diary	Berguette	25/11/1915	30/11/1915
Heading	12th Div 69th F.C.R.E. Vol.4		
War Diary	Berguette	01/12/1915	09/12/1915
War Diary	Gorre	10/12/1915	31/12/1915
Heading	12th Div 69th F.C.R.E. Vol: 5		
War Diary	Gorre	01/01/1916	15/01/1916
War Diary	L'Ecleme.	16/01/1916	29/01/1916
War Diary	Ligny	30/01/1916	30/01/1916
War Diary	L'Ecleme	31/01/1916	14/02/1916
War Diary	Sailly-La-Bourse	15/02/1916	29/02/1916
Heading	69 FCRE Vol 7		
War Diary	Sailly-La-Bourse	01/03/1916	23/03/1916
War Diary	Philosophe	24/03/1916	24/04/1916
War Diary	Burbure	25/04/1916	07/05/1916
War Diary	Maroc	08/05/1916	25/05/1916
War Diary	Burbure	01/06/1916	12/06/1916
War Diary	Frechencourt	13/06/1916	13/06/1916
War Diary	St. Gratien	14/06/1916	30/06/1916
War Diary	Coyecque	26/06/1916	27/06/1916
War Diary	Burbure	28/06/1916	31/06/1916
Heading	War Diary 69th Field Coy. Period 1-7-16-31-7-16		
War Diary	Bresle	01/07/1916	06/07/1916
War Diary	Aveluy Defences	07/07/1916	08/07/1916
War Diary	Vadencourt.	09/07/1916	10/07/1916
War Diary	Bus-Les-Artois	11/07/1916	18/07/1916
War Diary	Mailly Mallet	19/07/1916	19/07/1916
War Diary	Bus-Les-Artois	20/07/1916	20/07/1916

War Diary	Mailly Mallet	21/07/1916	24/07/1916
War Diary	Bouzincourt	25/07/1916	31/07/1916
Heading	War Diary of 69th Field Coy. R.E. From 31-7-16 To 30-8-16 Vol 12		
War Diary	Near Aveluy W. 12 D. 7 2	01/08/1916	12/08/1916
War Diary	Bouzincourt.	13/08/1916	16/08/1916
War Diary	Authiele.	17/08/1916	17/08/1916
War Diary	Liencourt	18/08/1916	21/08/1916
War Diary	Arras.	22/08/1916	31/08/1916
Heading	War Diary of 69th Field Coy. Royal Engineers From 30-8-16 To 29-9-16 Vol 13		
War Diary	Arras.	01/09/1916	27/09/1916
War Diary	Milly	28/09/1916	30/09/1916
Heading	War Diary 69th Field Company. Royal Engineers For Month Ending 31st October.		
War Diary	Pommiers.	01/10/1916	01/10/1916
War Diary	Longueval	02/10/1916	19/10/1916
War Diary	Fricourt	20/10/1916	29/10/1916
War Diary	Dernan-Court	30/10/1916	30/10/1916
War Diary	Talmas.	31/10/1916	31/10/1916
Heading	War Diary November 1916 69th Field Coy RE Vol 15		
War Diary	Near Doullens.	01/11/1916	01/11/1916
War Diary	Gouy	02/11/1916	04/11/1916
War Diary	Arras.	05/11/1916	16/12/1916
War Diary	Duisans.	17/12/1916	17/12/1916
War Diary	Lignereuil	18/12/1916	31/12/1916
Heading	War Diary of 69th Field Coy., R.E. From 1-1-17 To 31-7-17 Vol 17		
War Diary	Lignereuil	01/01/1917	31/01/1917
Heading	War Diary of 69th Field Coy. R.E. From 1.2.1917 to 28.2.1917 (Volume 21)		
War Diary	Lignereuil	01/02/1917	05/02/1917
War Diary	Arras.	06/02/1917	28/02/1917
Heading	War Diary of 69th Field Coy. R.E. From 1.3.17 to 31.3.17 (Volume 22)		
War Diary	Arras.	01/03/1917	24/03/1917
Heading	War Diary of 69th Field Coy. R.E. From 1.4.1917 To 30.4.1917 (Volume 23)		
War Diary	Arras.	01/04/1917	11/04/1917
War Diary	Near Peuchy-Capiel.	12/04/1917	12/04/1917
War Diary	Arras	13/04/1917	24/04/1917
War Diary	Feuchy	25/04/1917	30/04/1917
Heading	War Diary of 69th Field Coy. R.E. From 1.5.17 To 31.5.17 (Volume 24)		
War Diary	Railway Triangle	01/05/1917	15/05/1917
War Diary	Arras.	16/05/1917	18/05/1917
War Diary	Simencourt	19/05/1917	23/05/1917
War Diary	Ivergny	24/05/1917	31/05/1917
Heading	War Diary of 69th Field Coy RE From 1.6.17 to 30.6.17 (Volume 25)		
War Diary	Ivergny N.21.d.5.2	01/06/1917	16/06/1917
War Diary	Arras.	17/06/1917	17/06/1917
War Diary	Nr. Tilloy	18/06/1917	30/06/1917
Heading	War Diary of 69th Field Coy R.E. From 1.7.17 To 31.7.17 Volume (26)		
War Diary	51 D N.2.d.5.7. Near Tilloy	01/07/1917	31/07/1917

Heading	War Diary of 69th Field Coy RE From 1.8.17 To 31.8.17 (Volume 27)		
War Diary	Nr. Tilloy N.2.d.5.7.	01/08/1917	31/08/1917
Heading	Dugouts		
Heading	War Diary of 69th Field Company. R.E. From 31.8.17 To 29.9.17 Vol 28		
War Diary	Near Tilloy N.2.d.5.7.	01/09/1917	21/10/1917
War Diary	Hauteville	22/10/1917	22/10/1917
War Diary	Gde Rullecourt	23/10/1917	27/10/1917
War Diary	Rebreuve	28/10/1917	28/10/1917
War Diary	Blangermont	29/10/1917	31/10/1917
Heading	War Diary of 69th Field Coy. R.E. From 1.11.17 To 29.11.17 (Volume 30).		
War Diary	Blangermont	01/11/1917	15/11/1917
War Diary	Moislains	16/11/1917	16/11/1917
War Diary	Heudicourt.	17/11/1917	19/11/1917
War Diary	Villers-Guislain.	20/11/1917	29/11/1917
Heading	War Diary of 69th Field Coy R.E. From 29.11.17 To 31.12.17 Vol 28		
War Diary	Heudicourt	30/11/1917	04/12/1917
War Diary	Cartigny	05/12/1917	05/12/1917
War Diary	Bouzincourt	06/12/1917	07/12/1917
War Diary	Witternesse	08/12/1917	10/12/1917
War Diary	Guarbecque	11/12/1917	12/12/1917
War Diary	Houleron	13/12/1917	25/12/1917
War Diary	Merville	26/12/1917	26/12/1917
War Diary	Les 3 Tilleuls	27/12/1917	31/12/1917
Heading	12th Divisional Engineers 69th Field Company R.E. January 1918		
Heading	War Diary of 69th Field Coy R.E. From 1.1.18 31.1.18 (Volume 32)		
War Diary	Les. 3 Tilleuls Nr. Armentieres.	01/01/1918	15/01/1918
War Diary	Fort Rompu	16/01/1918	31/01/1918
Heading	12th Divisional Engineers 69th Field Company R.E. February 1918		
Heading	War Diary of 69th Field Coy R.E. 1.2.18 To 28.2.18 (Volume 33)		
War Diary	Fort Rompu H. 13 b. 3.6.	01/02/1918	28/02/1918
Heading	12th Divisional Engineers War Diary 69th Field Company R.E. March 1918		
Heading	War Diary of 69th Field Coy R.E. From 1.3.18 31.3.18 Vol 31		
War Diary	Fort Rompu H. 13 B 3 6	01/03/1918	20/03/1918
War Diary	Erquinghem H 8 B 10 3	20/03/1918	24/03/1918
War Diary	Oblinghem	24/03/1918	25/03/1918
War Diary	Bouzincourt	26/03/1918	28/03/1918
War Diary	Hedauville	29/03/1918	29/03/1918
War Diary	Warloy	30/03/1918	31/03/1918
Heading	12th Div. 69th Field Company, R.E. April 1918		
War Diary	57D. 1/40000 Warloy	01/04/1918	02/04/1918
War Diary	Senlis	03/04/1918	11/04/1918
War Diary	57D. 1/40000 Warloy.	12/04/1918	24/04/1918
War Diary	Acheux	25/04/1918	30/04/1918
Heading	12th Divisional Engineers 69th Field Company R.E. May 1918		

Heading	War Diary of 69th Field Coy. RE From 1/5/18 31/5/18 (Volume 36)		
War Diary	Sheet 57D 1/40000 Acheux	01/05/1918	13/05/1918
War Diary	Beaussart	14/05/1918	25/05/1918
War Diary	Puchevillers	26/05/1918	27/05/1918
Heading	12th Divisional Engineers 69th Field Company R.E. June 1918		
Heading	War Diary 69th Field Coy R.E. From 1.6.18 To 29.6.18 (Volume 37)		
War Diary	Sheet 57D 1/40000 Pucheyillers.	01/06/1918	01/06/1918
War Diary	Acheux	02/06/1918	03/06/1918
War Diary	Puchevillers	05/06/1918	17/06/1918
War Diary	Camp. V.2.D. 4.6	18/06/1918	29/06/1918
Heading	12th Divisional Engineers 69th Field Company R.E. July 1918		
Heading	War Diary of 69th Field Coy RE From 30.6.18 To 30.7.18 (Volume 38)		
War Diary	57D. 1/40000 Y. 2.d. Near Hedauville	30/06/1918	09/07/1918
War Diary	Rubempre	10/07/1918	13/07/1918
War Diary	Namps aumont Rumigny.	14/07/1918	15/07/1918
War Diary	Amiens. Sheet 17 Rumigny.	16/07/1918	29/07/1918
War Diary	Lens. II Havernas	30/07/1918	30/07/1918
Heading	12th Divisional Engineers 69th Field Company, Royal Engineers, August, 1918.		
War Diary	Havernas.	31/07/1918	02/08/1918
War Diary	(Sheet Lens. II). 62D. 1/40000 D. 19 a. 3 2 Nr. Baizieux	03/08/1918	10/08/1918
War Diary	J S 6 7 5 Nr. Mericourt.	11/08/1918	22/08/1918
War Diary	62D 1/40000 K.1.d.2.6 Near Morlancourt	23/08/1918	25/08/1918
War Diary	E.12.d.8.5 Becordel Becourt	26/08/1918	30/09/1918
Miscellaneous	12th Divisional Engineers 69th Field Company R.E. September 1918		
Miscellaneous	War Diary of 69th Field Coy RE (Volume 40)		
War Diary	E.12.d.8.5 Bercodel-Becourt	31/08/1918	03/09/1918
War Diary	Fregicourt. T. 29.b. 9.7	04/09/1918	05/09/1918
War Diary	Hennois Wood.	06/09/1918	06/09/1918
War Diary	D. 2 C. 8.2 W. of Nurlu.	07/09/1918	16/09/1918
War Diary	Dismounted. E.14.C.5. Mounted to West of Lieramont.	17/09/1918	17/09/1918
War Diary	E. 14 C. 5 5 W of Lieramont.	18/09/1918	22/09/1918
War Diary	C 4 C 8 8 W of Epehy	23/09/1918	30/09/1918
Heading	12th Divisional Engineers 69th Field Company R.E. October 1918		
Heading	War Diary of 69th Field Coy R.E. Oct 1st To Oct 31st 1918 Vol 38		
War Diary		01/10/1918	31/10/1918
Heading	12th Divisional Engineers 69th Field Company R.E. November 1918		
Heading	War Diary of 69th Field Coy RE From 1.11.18 30.11.18 (Volume 42)		
War Diary		01/11/1918	30/11/1918
Heading	12th Divisional Engineers 69th Field Company R.E. December 1918		
Heading	War Diary of 69th Field Coy RE From 1.12.18 To 31.12.18 (Volume 42)		
War Diary	Aniche	01/12/1918	31/12/1918

Heading	War Diary of 69th Field Coy RE From 1.1.19 To 31.1.19 (Volume 44)		
War Diary	Aniche	01/01/1919	31/01/1919
Heading	War Diary of 69th Field Coy RE From 1.2.19 To 28.2.19 (Volume 44)		
War Diary	Aniche	01/02/1919	28/02/1919
War Diary	War Diary of 69th Field Coy R.E. From 1.3.19 To 31.3.19 (Volume 46)		
War Diary	Aniche	01/03/1919	31/03/1919
Heading	War Diary of 69th Field Coy R.E. From 1.4.19 To 30.4.19 (Volume 47)		
War Diary	Aniche	01/04/1919	30/04/1919
Heading	War Diary of 69th Field Coy RE From 1/5/19 To 31/5/19 (Volume 48)		
War Diary	Aniche France.	01/05/1919	31/05/1919
Heading	1840/2 70th Field Coy R.E.		
Heading	12th Division 70th Field Coy R.E. May 1915-May 1919		
Heading	12th Division 70th F.C.R.E. Vol. I. From May to Oct. 15		
Heading	War Diary of 70th Field Company R.E. from May 31st 1915 to Oct 31st 1915 (Volume 1)		
War Diary	70th Coy RE	01/06/1915	31/08/1915
Miscellaneous	Portable Search Light Ref G.305/CRE 1206	30/07/1915	30/07/1915
Miscellaneous			
Miscellaneous	Ref. CRE 889 Brigade Workshops.		
Miscellaneous	Brigade Workshops	30/07/1915	30/07/1915
War Diary		25/09/1915	30/10/1915
Miscellaneous	C.R.E. 12th Divn	20/10/1915	20/10/1915
Heading	12 Div 70th F.C.R.E. Vol. 2		
Heading	70th Field Coy R.E. War Diary for November & December 1915		
War Diary		01/11/1915	30/11/1915
Miscellaneous	Marching Out State for 70th Coy R.E. from Annequin. 14.11.15	14/11/1915	14/11/1915
War Diary		01/12/1915	31/12/1915
Heading	Marching Out State of 70th Fd. Coy R.E. from Annezin. 11.12.15	11/12/1915	11/12/1915
Miscellaneous	12th 70th F.C.R.E. Vol: 3 Jan 16		
Heading	War Diary of 70th Field Company R.E. from January 1, 1916 to January 31, 1916		
War Diary	Festubert. (Bullets at Gorre Brewery)	01/01/1916	18/01/1916
War Diary	Bourecq	01/01/1916	31/01/1916
Heading	War Diary for the month of February 1916 70th Field Company Royal Engineers		
War Diary	Bourecq	01/02/1916	11/02/1916
War Diary	Philosophe	12/02/1916	29/02/1916
Miscellaneous			
Heading	Original of War Diary of 70th Field Company Royal Engineers from March 1st 1916 to March 31st 1916		
War Diary	Philosophe	01/03/1916	31/03/1916
Miscellaneous	C.R.E. 12th Divn.	04/03/1916	04/03/1916
Operation(al) Order(s)	70th Field Co R.E. Operation Orders No.1 by Captain S.W.S. Hamilton R.E.	01/03/1916	01/03/1916
Heading	War Diary of 70th Field Company Royal Engineers from April 1st 1916 To April 30th 1916 Volume 8		
War Diary	Philosophe	01/04/1916	25/04/1916

War Diary	Haut Rieux	26/04/1916	30/04/1916
Heading	War Diary 70th Field Coy R.E. for Period May 1st 1916 to 31st 1916 Volume 9		
War Diary	Mazingarbe Haut Meux	01/05/1916	31/05/1916
Heading	War Diary 70th Field Coy R.E. for Period 1.6.16-30.6.16 Volume 10		
War Diary	Mazingarbe	01/06/1916	30/06/1916
Heading	War Diary 70th Field Coy R.E. Period 1.7.16-31.7.16 Volume II		
War Diary	Field	01/07/1916	31/07/1916
Heading	War Diary (Original) 70th Field Coy R.E. Volume 12 August 1st-31st 1916		
War Diary	Bougaincourt and Aveluy	01/08/1916	26/08/1916
War Diary	Agny	26/08/1916	31/08/1916
Heading	War Diary 70th Field Coy R.E. for Period. Sept. 1st 1916-Sept 30th 1916 Volume.13		
War Diary	Agny	01/09/1916	26/09/1916
War Diary	Warlus	26/09/1916	26/09/1916
War Diary	Milly	27/09/1916	29/09/1916
War Diary	War Diary 70th Field Coy R.E. for Period. October 1st 1916-Oct 31st 1916 Volume 14		
War Diary	Field	01/10/1916	31/10/1916
Heading	War Diary 70th Field Company R.E. for period Nov. 1st 1916-Nov. 30th 1916 Volume 15		
War Diary	Field	30/10/1916	02/11/1916
War Diary	Gouy	03/11/1916	04/11/1916
War Diary	Agny	05/11/1916	30/11/1916
Heading	War Diary 70th Field Company R.E. Vol. 16 Period 1.12.16-31.12.16		
War Diary	Field	01/12/1916	31/12/1916
Heading	War Diary 70th Field Company R.E. for period 1.1.17 to 31.1.17 Vol. 17		
War Diary	Field	01/01/1917	31/01/1917
Heading	War Diary 70th Field Company R.E. Period 1.2.17-28.2.17 Volume 18		
War Diary	Arras	01/02/1917	28/02/1917
Heading	War Diary 70th Field Company R.E. for period 1.3.17 to 31.3.17 Volume 19		
War Diary	Arras.	01/03/1917	31/03/1917
Heading	War Diary 70th Field Company. R.E. for period 1.4.17 to 30.4.17 Volume 20		
War Diary	Arras	01/04/1917	10/04/1917
War Diary	Feuchy Chapel	11/04/1917	11/04/1917
War Diary	Rouville	12/04/1917	13/04/1917
War Diary	Noyellette	14/04/1917	14/04/1917
War Diary	Mondicourt	15/04/1917	22/04/1917
War Diary	Wauquetim	23/04/1917	23/04/1917
War Diary	Arras	24/04/1917	25/04/1917
War Diary	Railway	26/04/1917	29/04/1917
War Diary	Feuchy	30/04/1917	30/04/1917
War Diary	War Diary of 70th Field Co. R.E. from May 1, 1917 to May 31, 1917 Volume 21		
War Diary	Feuchy	01/05/1917	12/05/1917
War Diary	Arras	16/05/1917	16/05/1917
War Diary	Gouves	17/05/1917	23/05/1917
War Diary	Ivergny	24/05/1917	31/05/1917

Heading	War Diary of 70th Field Coy R.E. from June 1, 1917 to June 30, 1917 Volume 22		
War Diary	Ivergny	01/06/1917	16/06/1917
War Diary	Gouves	17/06/1917	17/06/1917
War Diary	Arras	18/06/1917	18/06/1917
War Diary	In the Field	19/06/1917	30/06/1917
Heading	War Diary of 70th Field Co. R.E. from July 1, 1917 to July 31, 1917 Volume 23		
War Diary	In the Field	01/07/1917	31/07/1917
Heading	War Diary of 70th Field Co. R.E. from Aug. 1. 1917 to Aug. 31, 1917 Volume 24		
War Diary	In the Field	01/08/1917	31/08/1917
Heading	War Diary of 70th Field Co. R.E. from Sep. 1, 1917 to Sep 30, 1917 Volume 25		
War Diary	In the Field	01/09/1917	30/09/1917
Heading	War Diary of 70th Field Co. R.E. October 1, 1917 to October 31, 1917 Volume 26		
War Diary	In the Field	01/10/1917	31/10/1917
Heading	War Diary of 70th Field Co. R.E. from Nov. 1, 1917 to Nov. 29, 1917 Volume 27		
War Diary	In the Field	01/11/1917	29/11/1917
Heading	War Diary of 70th Fd Co. R.E. from Dec. 1, 1917 to Dec. 31, 1917 Volume 28		
War Diary		03/12/1917	27/12/1917
War Diary		30/11/1917	02/12/1917
Heading	12th Divisional Engineers 70th Field Company R.E. January 1918		
Heading	War Diary of 70th Fd. Co. R.E. from Jan 1, 1918 to Jan 31, 1918 Volume 29		
War Diary	Armentieres	01/01/1918	16/01/1918
War Diary	Nouveau Monde	17/01/1918	31/01/1918
Heading	12th Divisional Engineers 70th Field Company R.E. February 1918		
Heading	War Diary of 70th Fd. Coy. R.E. from Feb. 1, 1918 to Feb 28, 1918 Volume 30		
War Diary		01/02/1918	28/02/1918
Heading	12th Divisional Engineers. War Diary 70th Field Company R.E. March 1918		
Heading	War Diary of 70th Fd Coy R.E. from March 1st 1918 to March 31st 1918 Volume 31		
War Diary	Bac St Maur	01/03/1918	31/03/1918
Heading	12th Div. 70th Field Company, R.E. April 1918		
Heading	War Diary of 70th Fd Co. R.E. from 1st April 1918 to 30th April 1918 Volume 32		
War Diary	Warloy	01/04/1918	02/04/1918
War Diary	Senlis	03/04/1918	11/04/1918
War Diary	Warloy	12/04/1918	24/04/1918
War Diary	Acheux	25/04/1918	30/04/1918
Heading	12th Divisional Engineers 70th Field Company R.E. May 1918		
War Diary	War Diary of 70th Field Coy R.E. from 1st May 1918 to 31st May 1918 Volume 33		
War Diary	In & near Acheux	01/05/1918	31/05/1918
Heading	12th Divisional Engineers 70th Field Company R.E. June 1918		

Heading	War Diary of 70th Field Coy R.E. from June 1st 1918 to June 30th 1918 Volume 34		
War Diary	Beauquesne	01/06/1918	30/06/1918
Heading	12th Divisional Engineers 70th Field Company R.E. July 1918		
Heading	War Diary of 70th Fd Coy R.E. from July 1, 1918 to July 31, 1918 Volume 35		
War Diary	Near Senlis	01/07/1918	10/07/1918
War Diary	Toutencourt	11/07/1918	15/07/1918
War Diary	Flers	16/07/1918	30/07/1918
War Diary	Vignacourt	31/07/1918	31/07/1918
Heading	12th Divisional Engineers 70th Field Company. Royal Engineers. August, 1918.		
Heading	War Diary of 70th Field Company R.E. August 1st 1918 to August 31st 1918 Volume 36		
War Diary	Vignacourt	01/08/1918	02/08/1918
War Diary	Ribemont	03/08/1918	22/08/1918
War Diary	Ville	23/08/1918	25/08/1918
War Diary	Becordel	26/08/1918	29/08/1918
War Diary	Mametz	30/08/1918	31/08/1918
Heading	12th Divisional Engineers 70th Field Company R.E. September 1918		
Heading	War Diary of 70th Field Company R.E. September 1st 1918 to September 30th 1918 Volume 37		
War Diary	Mametz	01/09/1918	04/09/1918
War Diary	Combles	04/09/1918	05/09/1918
War Diary	Manancourt	06/09/1918	06/09/1918
War Diary	Lieramont	17/09/1918	29/09/1918
Heading	12th Divisional Engineers 70th Field Company R.E. October 1918		
Heading	War Diary of 70th Field Co R.E. Oct. 1, 1918 to Oct. 31, 1918 Volume 38		
War Diary	Liermont	01/10/1918	01/10/1918
War Diary	Merignolls	03/10/1918	03/10/1918
War Diary	Chateau	04/10/1918	04/10/1918
War Diary	De La Haie Vimy	05/10/1918	11/10/1918
War Diary	Sallaumines	12/10/1918	14/10/1918
War Diary	Dourges	17/10/1918	18/10/1918
War Diary	Courtiches	19/10/1918	19/10/1918
War Diary	Landas	21/10/1918	21/10/1918
War Diary	Lecelles	24/10/1918	28/10/1918
War Diary	Rue De Rosult.	29/10/1918	31/10/1918
Heading	12th Divisional Engineers 70th Field Company R.E. November 1918		
Heading	War Diary of 70th Field Co R.E. Nov. 1 1918 to Nov 30 1918 Volume 39		
War Diary	Rosult	01/11/1918	07/11/1918
War Diary	Odomez	08/11/1918	11/11/1918
War Diary	Stambruges	12/11/1918	25/11/1918
War Diary	St Amand	25/11/1918	25/11/1918
War Diary	Aniche	26/11/1918	30/11/1918
Heading	12th Divisional Engineers 70th Field Company R.E. December 1918		
Heading	War Diary of 70th Field Co. R.E. Dec. 1, 1918 to Dec. 31, 1918 Volume 40		
War Diary	Aniche.	01/12/1918	31/12/1918

Heading	War Diary of 70th Field Co. Royal Engineers from Jan 1 1919 to Jan 31 1919 Volume 41		
War Diary	Aniche	01/01/1919	31/01/1919
Heading	War Diary of 70th Field Coy. Royal Engineers From Feb. 1st. 1919 to Feb 28th 1919 Volume 42		
War Diary	Aniche	01/02/1919	28/02/1919
Heading	War Diary of 70th Field Company R.E. from Mar. 1, 1919 to Mar 31, 1919 Volume 43		
War Diary	Aniche	01/03/1919	31/03/1919
Heading	War Diary of 70th Field Co R.E. from April 1 1919 to April 30 1919 Volume 44		
War Diary	Aniche	01/04/1919	30/04/1919
Heading	War Diary of 70th Field Co R.E. from May 1 1919 to May 10 1919 Volume 45		
War Diary	Aniche	01/05/1919	10/05/1919

1840/1
64th Field Coy R.E.

12TH DIVISION

69TH FIELD COY. R.E.
MAY
JUN 1915 - MAY 1919

121/7753

13th Division

69th F.C.R.E.
Vol I

June, July, Aug, & Sep/15

Army Form C. 2118

Instructions regarding War Diaries and Intelligence
Summaries are contained in F. S. Regs., Part II.
and the Staff Manual respectively. Title pages
will be prepared in manuscript.

WAR DIARY
INTELLIGENCE SUMMARY.
(Erase heading not required.)

Place	Date	Hour	Summary of Events and Information	Remarks and references to Appendices
ALDERSHOT	31/5		6 Officers & 222 O.R. entrained at FARNBOROUGH for SOUTHAMPTON with full transport.	
SOUTHAMPTON	"		" embarked at SOUTHAMPTON for HAVRE	
HAVRE	1/6		" arrived at HAVRE Rest camp.	
"	2/6		" entrained for ST OMER.	
ST OMER	3/6		" arrived at ST OMER & billeted 3 miles south of ST OMER. (WIZERNES)	
WIZ	4/6			
"	5/6		Marched from WIZ to CINQ-RUES. Brigaded as part of 36 F. Brigade	
CINQ-RUES	6/6		" CINQ RUES to NOOT BOOM	
NOOT BOOM	7/6		" NOOT BOOM to ERQUINGHEM. Up to and including 6/6 worked as part of 36 F. Coy. R.E. XII Div. From today, worked with No 2 & No 3 Coy of Divisional Engineers directly under C.R.E. XII Div.	
ERQUINGHEM	8/6		Rest day.	
"	9/6		6 Company instructed by R.E. in use of respirator	
"	10/6		Attached to 17th Coy. R.E. for instruction in Wire & Trenches at ARMENTIERES.	
"	11/6			
"	12/6			
"	13/6			
"	14/6		Marched to LE VERRIER. 6 Draws Horses & mules attached to 116 F Coy. A.S.C.	
LE VERRIER	15/6			
"	16/6		Drawing Orders	
"	17/6		Bridge Building instruction	
"	18/6		Marched to ERQUINGHEM	
"	19/6			
ERQUINGHEM	20/6		2 Sections marched to PLOEGSTEERT WOOD. Remainder 1 mile south of PLOEGSTEERT.	

G.F. Vance
COMMANDING 69th (FIELD) COMPANY R.E.

WAR DIARY
INTELLIGENCE SUMMARY.
(Erase heading not required.)

Army Form C. 21

Instructions regarding War Diaries and Intelligence Summaries are contained in F. S. Regs., Part II. and the Staff Manual respectively. Title pages will be prepared in manuscript.

Place	Date	Hour	Summary of Events and Information	Remarks and references to Appendices
PLOEGSTEERT	20/9/15		2 Sections employed at night with 600 m. Jow Bns digging communication trench	
	21/9/15		2 " " putting localities in to state of defence	
	22/9/15		Ditto. 1st Casualty Pond Sapr. T. Shell wound while in Bivouac	
	23 "			
	24 "		As on the 20 & 21st	
	25 "		1 & 2 Sections rejoined H.Q. Capt. Gosport with 3 & 4 Sections took over trenches Posts of Pinet Ky. 8.	
	26 "		Relief with infantry on 3 reference localities	
	27 "		Nil	
	28 "		Relieving over trenches. Self reconnoitering. Work on a defence locality	
	29 "		Work on Hd. Defensive locality. Self reconnoitering. Messing with No 2 Section Officer. Carrying out communication trench	
	30 "		Carrying material. Though digging Communication trench.	

(signature)
MAJOR, R.E.
COMMANDING 69th (FIELD) COMPANY R.E.

WAR DIARY
INTELLIGENCE SUMMARY

Army Form C. 2118

Place	Date	Hour	Summary of Events and Information	Remarks and references to Appendices
PLOEGSTEERT	1/5		Building bomb shelter, report on the whereabouts of communication trenches. 1st Lt Regent. Communication trench. Digging wire on fire trench with infantry. Grenade ditto.	
	2"		Drawing stores. Improving communication trench as yesterday.	
	3"			
	4"		Rev. Communication trench. Laying out support trench. Digging wire jam tin on S.F.T.	
	5"			
	6"			
ARMENTIERES	9th		Day & night on 2nd line trench (= com. trench)	
	10"			
	11"			
	2"		Started a new Avenue (Avenue = Communication trench)	
	08"		" " " " "	
	4"		" " " " "	
	5"		working on the new Avenue	

G.S. Minor
MAJOR, R.E.
COMMANDING 65th (FIELD) COMPANY R.E.

Army Form C. 2118

WAR DIARY
or
INTELLIGENCE SUMMARY.
(Erase heading not required.)

Instructions regarding War Diaries and Intelligence Summaries are contained in F. S. Regs., Part II. and the Staff Manual respectively. Title pages will be prepared in manuscript.

Place	Date	Hour	Summary of Events and Information	Remarks and references to Appendices
ARMENTIERES.	1/15 8		Constructing a support firing trench along S.4 & B5 & Rue Boret. Also 3 communication trenches. Ditto S.F.T. Rifle Gm. & trenches. Work with Belgian Inf. on subsidiary line	
	2 "		Various Duties	
	3 "		Support firing trenches for Royal Engineers & trenches only	
	4 "		S.F.T. 3 Com. trenches. Advanced sap at Lt. TOUQUET & Machine Gun emplacement. Subsidiary Line with Belgians.	
	5 "		As on the 5th. Also 2 covered mines	
	6 "		Work on support file trenches. Bank work, Machine Gun emplacement, making loopholes & various subsidiary line, tied up in wired to render field of many Brigade Battle H.Qrs., wires supply (pumping from well) & making Communication Trenches.	
	7/8 "			
	9 "			
	10 "			
	11 to 31 "			

E. ?. ?.
MAJOR, R.E.
COMMANDING 60th (FIELD) COMPANY R.E.

WAR DIARY
INTELLIGENCE SUMMARY

Army Form C. 2118

Instructions regarding War Diaries and Intelligence Summaries are contained in F.S. Regs., Part II. and the Staff Manual respectively. Title pages will be prepared in manuscript.

Place	Date	Hour	Summary of Events and Information	Remarks and references to Appendices
ARMENTIERES.	Sept. 1st to 8		One section detached for drainage works G.H.Q. Principal works of remainder. Construction of Vickers gun emplacement with bed available. Lofts for loans. Dugbag communication trenches. Laying Eunvails (wooden) for plating ricochets. Knocking slating Louts.	
"	10 to 23		One section detached for drainage. G.H.Q. Principal works of remainder. Vickers Dugouts, communication trenches, wooden tramway, knocking slating Louts & tool forge for Brigade and Battalion & Glos. V. Brigade H.Q.	
"	24		Standing by waiting for orders.	
"	25		Arranged for attack on trench systems. Remained in reserve.	
"	26		Recommenced work at at the beginning of week.	
"	27		5 p.m. orders to be ready to march.	
"	28		Standing by to march. Concentrated the Coy.	
"	29		Mounted men & Transport by road. Remainder of Coy by road & Tram to VANTRICOURT S.W. of BETHUNE	
"	30		Marched to billets N. of MAZINGARBE.	

G.S. Major
MAJOR, R.E.
COMMANDING 69th (FIELD) COMPANY R.E.

121/7518

13th Hussars

69th F.C.R.E.
Vol: 2

Oct 15

WAR DIARY / INTELLIGENCE SUMMARY

Army Form C. 2118.

Place	Date	Hour	Summary of Events and Information	Remarks and references to Appendices
VERMELLES	1 OCT 1915		Daylight. Reconnoitred roads & advanced trenches. Night, blew up subsidiary thereunto.	
	2 OCT 1915		Making trip-self-entanglements in billets.	
	3 OCT 1915		Ditto	
	4 OCT 1915		Ditto. 1 Infantry Divisional advanced reinforcement. Through billets in search of daylight.	
	5 OCT 1915		Transport sent to C.R.E. Divisional work was continued.	
	6 OCT 1915		Reshoring stores. Turned in left company. Took one line from 5 Coy R.E.	
	7 OCT 1915		Transport to C.R.E. & No 2 Section. Digging trench & carrying stores for same time.	
	8 OCT 1915		Transport sent to No 2 trench. Coys tied up & No 2 Section wiring in attack on enemy trench — a failure. General bombardment of XI Dur. Front	
	9 OCT 1915		Blowing up graves & 6 shells to Coy, 3 transports of stores.	
	10 OCT 1915		Wiped R.E. advanced 9 & 2nd Bde Wys, 3 shells thrown 2 Communication Trench.	
	11 OCT 1915		Using a trench & trenches of stores.	
	12 OCT 1915		Calling out & digging trenches. Making aid post. No 4 H.E. Transport sent to C.R.E. La Bourse. Section borrowed somewhat killed & which were taken by day to + Co. all Officers & 4 Sections marched to trenches.	
EAST of VERMELLES	13 OCT 1915		No 1 & 2 Sections detailed to two 1st Batt with 1 battalion in attack on enemy trenches "S.4". In Reserve. Attack by 1st Battalion on German trench by Succeeded. No 1 Section helping English Trenches Corn & Trenches Consolidate position won. Shovel & Gabions etc. Forwarded by Coy to Trench.	
	14 OCT 1915		Soon after Midnight brought back to Capt. Oyster to No 1 Section back to reserve in billets in this dug-out. Relieved Co 2 Section before darkness night 13 and & Coys No 3 continued the work in the night fall	

A.S. Vivian
MAJOR, R.E.
COMMANDING 69th (FIELD) COMPANY R.E.

Army Form C. 2118.

WAR DIARY
or
INTELLIGENCE SUMMARY.
(Erase heading not required.)

Place	Date	Hour	Summary of Events and Information	Remarks and references to Appendices
EAST of VERMELLES	15 OCT 1915 to 18 OCT 1915		4 Sections engaged in work of repairing parapets, wiring & digging new telephone & communication trenches & R.E. work generally.	
	19 OCT 1915		Marched out to trenches at 7.30 a.m. picking up telephone Coy en route to a field at VANDRICOURT arriving about 2.30 p.m.	
VANDRICOURT	20 OCT 1915 to 23		Holidays at VANDRICOURT	
	24 OCT 1915		Inspected by General Officer Commanding XIth Div.	
	25 OCT 1915		Marched to billets in ANNEQUIN 9.30 a.m. to 3 p.m. (5 miles)	
ANNEQUIN	26 OCT 1915		Commenced Brigade C.G. Dug-outs.	
	27 OCT 1915		4 Sections on digging Bde C.G. Dug-out. Officers reconnoitring.	
	28 OCT 1915		No Dug-out work tough. detailed to Bde.R.E. Yesterday clearing Com. Trench	
	29 OCT 1915		The Dug-out Fort tough. Yesterday clearing Com. Trenches. Investigating repairs required to trenches & trench lines.	
	30 OCT 1915		Finished two sheets & most tough. Started 3 Front House Ja.R.P.M. Continued on the C.G. Dont-Loop, Com. Trenches: Investigating estimating for billeting sheds in Quisinch Brie.	
	31 OCT 1915		Work proceeding on various Comm. Progs & Com. Trenches. Sketches and estimates for billeting sheds, trench. Dugouts, cellars. Bde R.E. Transport &c.	

E.S. Kirn
MAJOR, R.E.
COMMANDING 69th (FIELD) COMPANY R.E.

Ogh. P.C. R.E.
Vol: 3

121/7678

13th Division

Nov 15

Army Form C. 2118.

WAR DIARY
or
INTELLIGENCE SUMMARY.
(Erase heading not required.)

Instructions regarding War Diaries and Intelligence Summaries are contained in F. S. Regs., Part II. and the Staff Manual respectively. Title pages will be prepared in manuscript.

Place	Date	Hour	Summary of Events and Information	Remarks and references to Appendices
ANNEQUIN	1 NOV 1915		Work in progress on Dugouts, Trench-name boards etc.	
	2 NOV 1915		As on the 1st. Additional Bomb Stores, Scaling ladders, Timber Platforms for Howitzers.	
	3 NOV 1915		" 2nd " Making O.P.s in ruins of & repairs demolished in addition	
	4 NOV 1915		Flooring barns, Hd Qr R.E. Dugout, various small dugouts, fixing Platforms for guns etc	
	5/6 NOV 1915		As on the 4th + 5th 9 Batt. Front.	
	8 NOV 1915		As on the 8th Brick observation tower. Taking over work in trenches from 87th Coy R.E.	
	9 NOV 1915		As on the 8th Hodgesaps, fixing signs, boards & arranging for work in front trenches near	
	10 NOV 1915		Bath House. HOHENZOLLERN REDOUBT. Making Bridge to C.	
	11 NOV 1915		HOHENZOLLERN REDOUBT. Trenches near HOHENZOLLERN REDOUBT, excavating Bath house at SAILLY LA BOURSE.	
	12 NOV 1915		Bomb-proofs, flooring saps, water supply, wire work & transport.	
	13		As on the 11th.	
	14 NOV 1915		As on the 11th Sub-two flooring of saps.	
	17 NOV 1915 /22		Bath house at LA BOURSE, in trenches dugouts, wire entanglements, repairing fire trenches, scraping trenches.	
	23 NOV 1915		As on the 17th till noon, when relieved by the 91st Coy. R.E.	
	24 NOV 1915		Mounted men by road, dismounted men by train to BEUVRILLES & BERGUETTE	
BERGUETTE	25 NOV 1915		Resting in billets.	
	26			
	27 NOV 1915		Renovating Farms BERGUETTE & district.	
	28 NOV 1915		Resting	
	29 NOV 1915		Renovating Farms BERGUETTE & district	
	30 NOV 1915			

E. S. Musson
MAJOR, R.E.
COMMANDING 69th (FIELD) COMPANY R.E.

69 h. 2. c. RE.
tot: 4

12/
7910

WAR DIARY
INTELLIGENCE SUMMARY.

(Erase heading not required.)

Army Form C. 2118.

Place	Date	Hour	Summary of Events and Information	Remarks and references to Appendices
BERGUETTE	1 DEC 1915		Renovating Farms etc in BERGUETTE and district	
	5 DEC 1915		Resting	
	6 DEC 1915		Renovating Farms etc in BERGUETTE and district	
	7		Inspection by C.R.E. & Fatigues	
	8 DEC 1915		Orders received at 8 P.M. to march to GORRE at 8.15 A.M. tomorrow	
	9 DEC 1915		Marched to billets 8.30 A.M. to 3 P.M. at GORRE.	
	10 DEC 1915		Reconnoitering Brigade area for work. Repairs to billets.	
	11 DEC 1915		Revetting Trenches & laying footboards. Improvements to billets.	
GORRE	12 DEC 1915		Studying main drainage. general maintenance of trenches.	
	13 DEC 1915		Drainage & work on billets.	
	14 DEC 1915		Ditto	
	15/16 DEC 1915		Ditto Working with 35 & 56 Bde and repairing Fontaine	
	17 DEC 1915			
	18 DEC 1915		Main Drainage, maintenance of trenches & improvement to billets	
	22 DEC 1915		Warned at 12.50 A.M. for repairs to front line. Having got there found hardly anything to do. Returned to billets 7.30 A.M. One section at work on maintenance of trenches.	
	23 DEC 1915		Main drainage & maintenance of trenches etc & work on billets.	
	24 DEC 1915			
	25 DEC 1915		" "	
	26 DEC 1915 to 31 DEC 1915		Main drainage, maintenance of trenches etc, work on billets, making revetments and floor boards.	

MAJOR, R.E.
COMMANDING 65th (FIELD) COMPANY R.E.

69th F.C. R.E.
Vol. 5

12th Div

Army Form C. 2118.

WAR DIARY
INTELLIGENCE SUMMARY.
(Erase heading not required.)

Place	Date	Hour	Summary of Events and Information	Remarks and references to Appendices
GORRE	1 JAN 1916		Drainage, Maintenance of trenches, making revetments & floorboards.	
	2 JAN 1916		" "	
	3		" "	
	4 JAN 1916		" "	
	5 JAN 1916		" , making floor boards	
	6 JAN 1916		" , making floor boards & revetment frames	
	7/8			
	9 JAN 1916		(Sunday) Rest	
	10 JAN 1916		Drainage Sgt. Gregory wounded. Maintenance of trenches, revetment frames & repairing dumps.	
	11 JAN 1916		Drainage, Maintenance of trenches & buildings, making revetment frames & repairing dumps	
	12/13/14		" "	
	15 JAN 1916		" Handed over to 5th Field Coy. R.E.	
L'ECLEME	16 JAN 1916		(Sunday) Marched 8.30 a.m - 12.30 p.m. 9 took over billets from 5 Fd. Coy R.E.	
	17 JAN 1916		Resting & improvements to billets	
	18/19		" "	
	20 JAN 1916		Drills. Overhauling kits, stores etc.	
	21/22		" "	
	23 JAN 1916		(Sunday) Church Parade. Fetching pontoons from Bridging Train.	
	24 JAN 1916		Pontooning Lab. drills.	
	25/26		" "	
	27 JAN 1916		Standing by to move at 2 hrs notice. 3 P.M. ordered to stand by	
	28 JAN 1916		Wire entanglements & demolitions	
	29 JAN 1916		"Standing by". Training in signalling knots & lashings & demolitions	
LIGNY	30 JAN 1916		Marched with XI Division & billeted at LIGNY-LES-AIRE	
L'ECLEME	31 JAN 1916		" Returned to billets at L'ECLEME } Manoeuvres	

A.S. ———
MAJOR, R.E.
COMMANDING 69th (FIELD) COMPANY R.E.

Army Form C. 2118.

WAR DIARY
or
INTELLIGENCE SUMMARY.
(Erase heading not required.)

Instructions regarding War Diaries and Intelligence Summaries are contained in F. S. Regs., Part II. and the Staff Manual respectively. Title pages will be prepared in manuscript.

Place	Date	Hour	Summary of Events and Information	Remarks and references to Appendices
L'ECLEME	1 FEB 1916		Drills, Wiring & Demolitions	
	2 FEB 1916		Drills & Pay	
	3 FEB 1916		Drills & Walking	
	4 FEB 1916		Drills, Inspection & Demolitions	
	5 FEB 1916		Cutting Bushwood	
	6 FEB 1916		Church Parade	
	7 FEB 1916		Rapt Exercise. Drills. Cutting bushwood	
	8 FEB 1916		Drills, Cutting bushwood. Inspection by G.O.C. on trip of N.C.O's & men mentioned	
	9 FEB 1916		Drills	
	10 FEB 1916		Lectures & inoculation	
	11 FEB 1916		Making weathervanes & inoculation	
	12/2			
	13 FEB 1916		& Church Parade	
	14 FEB 1916		Making & noticing Arrows, Racks for D.E. Pots Office, Cleaning of billets & Walking.	
SAILLY-LA-Bourse	15 FEB 1916		Coy marched to Sailly. No. 1 Section marched on to Philosophe.	
	16 FEB 1916		Works on Keeps & trenches & various small jobs.	
	17 FEB 1916			
	18 FEB 1916		As on 16th. The trenches are those W. & S. of the HOHENZOLLERN REDOUBT.	
	19 FEB 1916		" " 1 Man wounded	
	20 FEB 1916		" " 2 Men "	
	21 FEB 1916		" "	
	22 FEB 1916		" " Snow 2" deep.	
	23 FEB 1916		" " Add jobs in reserve, 3 Sections repairing keeps, benches etc. Snow	
	24 FEB 1916		as As at 23rd.	
	25/2			
	28 FEB 1916		" " 1 man wounded.	
	29 FEB 1916		" "	

E. S. Vinen
MAJOR, R.E.
COMMANDING 69th (FIELD) COMPANY R.E.

69 FERE
VOL 7

Army Form C. 2118.

WAR DIARY
or
INTELLIGENCE SUMMARY.

(Erase heading not required.)

Instructions regarding War Diaries and Intelligence Summaries are contained in F. S. Regs., Part II. and the Staff Manual respectively. Title pages will be prepared in manuscript.

Place	Date	Hour	Summary of Events and Information	Remarks and references to Appendices
SAILLY-LA-BOURSE	1 MAR 1916 4.		1 Section in H.E. yard. 3 Sections at PHILOSOPHE working on trenches, keeps & wiring.	
	5.	Sunday	1 Section in H.E. yard. 3 Sections working in craters W. of HOHENZOLLERN REDOUBT	
	6. "		After men in H.E. yard. 3 Sections working by Coy consolidating about craters.	
	7. "		Ditto. 1 Officer 18 O.R. standing by in order to help in attack on right of H.R. needed.	
	8. "		3 Section H.E. yard. Remainder consolidating craters.	
	9. "		Ditto. Right of 3/9 E. 1 Section under 2nd Lt Hodden took post for 2 hours in repelling	
			an attack. 1/9 Sergt Shepherd killed. Ptes Potters wounded.	
	10 "		½ Section H.E. yard. Remainder consolidating craters. Section under 2nd Lt Donald fifting	
			for 12 hours. Lt Hart & 4 O.R. wounded.	
	11/18		H.E. yard & craters consolidation.	
	19	Sunday	Right of 1/8/19 enemy took possession of all craters. All Coy out consolidating	
			Lt Hart wounded on 19th	
			H.E. yard. Consolidating sees lips of craters. 1 man wounded	
	20.		ditto	
	21		ditto	
	22		ditto	
PHILOSOPHE	23 24		Consolidation of craters. H.S moved to PHILOSOPHE. 1 O.R. wounded	
	25		" " Commenced entrances to deep dugouts. 2nd Lt J.C. Allemandes joined	
	26	Sunday	" " Construction of deep dug-outs	
	27		Ron 26? 1 O.R. 0. 910 men sapping all night. Offs. no less 2 mines.	
	28/31		Consolidation of craters H. Deep dugouts. Clearing trenches.	

E.S. ____
MAJOR, R.E.
COMMANDING 69th (FIELD) COMPANY R.E.

69 FCRE
Army Form C. 2118.
Vol 8

WAR DIARY
or
INTELLIGENCE SUMMARY.
(Erase heading not required.)

Place	Date	Hour	Summary of Events and Information	Remarks and references to Appendices
PHILOSOPHE	1st 4.16.		Consolidating craters. Deep Dug-outs.	
	2/4	"	" " "	
	3/4	"	" " "	
	5/8	"	Deep Dug-outs & staying at Crater "A"	
	9	Sunday	" " " "	
	10/15		Clearing WEST FACE of 2 craters where explosion	
			Deep Dug-outs only. 1 Sapper accidentally killed 13.4.16.	
	16		& cutting new support fire trench between MUD ALLEY & CROMWELL ROAD	
	17		Church Parade. Bathing Parade.	
	18		Deep Dug outs & cutting new support fire trench as on 16th. Working under 3rd Fdr.	
	19		Do on 16th. Clearing Cromwell the &c. support fire trench	
	20		" 19th. 1 N.C.O. wounded.	
	21		Deep Dug-outs. Excavating Sap 8A for loophole plate. Clearing trenches where newly cut by dug outs.	
	22/23		Do on 21st.	
	24		Deep Dugouts & cleaning up Killos Loading wagons.	
BURBURE	25		Mounted men by road & dismounted by train to Rest-billets at BURBURE 2½ miles SE LILLERS	
	26		Fatigues.	
	27		Drill. Consignment of German gas attack on Double Grassier the Coy. was standing by to move at ½ hours notice from 8.a.m. to 2.30 p.m.	
	28/29		Drills & Coy. training. Repairs to a large pump	
	30		Standing by from 6 p.m. 29th to 9 a.m. 30th	

E Ryan Lieut
MAJOR, R.E.
COMMANDING 69th (FIELD) COMPANY, R.E.

WAR DIARY
INTELLIGENCE SUMMARY
Army Form C. 2118.

66th Field Company, Royal Engineers

Place	Date	Hour	Summary of Events and Information	Remarks and references to Appendices
BURBURE	1.5.16		Route march Drills & fatigues.	
	2		Drills, bathing parade & fatigues.	
	3		Route march Drills & fatigues.	
	4		Drills, sports & fatigues.	
	5		Route March & fatigues	
	6		Drills	
	7		Fatigues & Horse.	
	8		Fatigues & Ho church parade owing to rain.	
MAROC	9		Company moved to MAROC. Dismounted to rest. Mounted the front.	
	10		Firing up hill 65. Setting out work & Posts of Kains & Logers. 1 NCO wounded.	
	11		Machine gun emplacements. Revetting Post-logging Repairs to billets. 1NCO & drivers killed, 2 drivers wounded.	
	12/15		Do on 10 " " " Trench torpedo exploded.	
	16		M.G. emplacements. Dugouts, wiring & post logging.	
	17/18		Do on 10 " Post Lieut knox relinquished command of Coy & Capt Jetaw assumes of R.D.& 5th Lieut.	
	19		" " "	
	20		Coy. march from MAROC into rest billets at BURBURE.	
	21		Drills & fatigues.	
	22		Drill.	
	23		4 Sections & gen Serv & Forge carts moved to Coycique for work on Boyskenvere line.	
			Nos Gens Nos Service at RU Rou R.E.	
			4 Sections in entrenchments at COYECQUE.	
	24		ditto C.R.E. at BURBURE. Rifle inspection.	
	25		ditto ditto Lorries arrived from base.	
			Ho 8th Ferval inspection	

E Mar Lieut
Commanding 66th (Field) Company R.E.

June 5

Army Form C. 2118.

Instructions regarding War Diaries and Intelligence Summaries are contained in F.S. Regs., Part II. and the Staff Manual respectively. Title pages will be prepared in manuscript.

WAR DIARY
INTELLIGENCE SUMMARY.
(Erase heading not required.)

Place	Date	Hour	Summary of Events and Information	Remarks and references to Appendices
BURBURE	1.6.1916.		Drills & Musketry. Standing-to to move at 4 hours notice from 8am to 5pm and 2 hours from 5pm to 8am.	
	2.6.		Captain J.J. Darlington R.E. took over command of the Coy. to-day. Drills & Musketry. Regimental Rifle competition in the morning	
	3.		Drills & Physical Drills.	
	4		Inspection Physical Drill. Regimental Sports in the afternoon	
	5		Route March & Bathing Parade. Musical Chairs & Inspection of Church Parade.	
	6		Lectures on Knotting, Lashing & Demolitions. Drill with arms & Physical Drill.	
	7/8		2 Sections practical in Knotting, Lashing & preparing Equipment & Demolitions.	
	9/10		Bathing, Lashing Gas helmets Inspection of same. Drill & Bombing.	
	11		Sketch & Bathing Parade.	
	12		Route March. Received orders to move.	
FRECHENCOURT	13		Moved 9 a.m. Marched to FOUQUEREUIL. Started entraining 12.15 p.m. finished 1.45 p.m. Train left 2.50. Reached LONGEAU near AMIENS at 10 - 1 am detrained by station midnight.	
	14		Marched to FRECHENCOURT. Wet March. Reached billets 4. 30 a.m. Moved at 4 - 7 pm for ST GRATIEN. Sailed and completed billets same day.	
ST GRATIEN	15		Employed under C.E.W. Corps. 2 Sections made 70 fascines, 2 Sections made II I loaded 50 ton wagons. Moved into permanent billets this day.	
	16.		Paraded 7.45 a.m. No.1 Section loading at FRECHENCOURT Stn. No. 2 Sect loading wagons in wood. No. 3 & 4 making 88 fascines.	

Major for Lieut Col R.E.
COMMANDING 68th (FIELD) COMPANY R.E.

Army Form C. 2118.

WAR DIARY
or
INTELLIGENCE SUMMARY.
(Erase heading not required.)

Instructions regarding War Diaries and Intelligence Summaries are contained in F. S. Regs., Part II. and the Staff Manual respectively. Title pages will be prepared in manuscript.

Place	Date	Hour	Summary of Events and Information	Remarks and references to Appendices
ST GRATIEN	17.6.16.		Paraded 7.45 am. Nos. 1, 3 & 4 on making fascines. No. 2 Sect. on cutting picks and loading waggons. Fine day. Fulton Waynshid 2 journeys to Stn.	
	18.		Paraded 7.45 am. 4 Sects. on fascines made 265. Fine day. Fulton Wagons made 2 journeys to Stn. G.T.M. Coys. came round about 7 ditches	
	19/6/		Paraded 7.45 a.m. 4 Sections on Fascines & loading.	
	22.		9a on 19t. O.C. & Offs. & N.C.O's proceeded to see portion of front line	
	23		with C.R.E. & returned in the afternoon.	
	24		9a on 19t. Further number of Offrs & N.C.O's went to see front line	
	25/26/		O.C. & Capt Alderdell conference at VIGNACOURT in afternoon	
	28			
	29		Inspections lectures etc under O.C. to Offs.	
			Coy. on cutting pickets, making fascines, digging half M.G. emplacements	
	30.		and laying out & supporting points.	
			Sections paraded for arms inspection, laying out strong points and Machine Gun emplacements etc.	

E Pease Lieut R.E.
for Capt. R.E.
COMMANDING 69th (FIELD) COMPANY R.E.

Army Form C. 2118.

WAR DIARY
INTELLIGENCE SUMMARY.
(Erase heading not required.)

Instructions regarding War Diaries and Intelligence Summaries are contained in F. S. Regs., Part II. and the Staff Manual respectively. Title pages will be prepared in manuscript.

Place	Date	Hour	Summary of Events and Information	Remarks and references to Appendices
COYECQUE	26.6.16.		4 Sections working on entrenchments at COYECQUE. H.Q'rs moved to COYECQUE.	
	27.		1 N.C.O. & 4 Drivers with 1 Pontoon & 1 Trestle Wagons to MAGNIEUX. Entrenchments. Orders received at 7.45 p.m. to move at once to BUSBURE. Coy. marched and arrived at BUSBURE at 8.20 a.m. on 28th	
BUSBURE	28.		Resting	
	29.		Drills. Starting to "b" from 11 a.m. at 1 hours notice.	
	30.		" to move at 1 hours notice	
	31.		" to move at 2 hours notice.	

F. Nach Lieut. R.E.
COMMANDING 69th (FIELD) COMPANY R.E.

12/
69. F.C. RE
Vol II

July

War Diary
69th Field Coy.

Period 1-7-16 — 31-7-16

WAR DIARY
or
INTELLIGENCE SUMMARY.
(Erase heading not required.)

Army Form C. 2118.

Place	Date	Hour	Summary of Events and Information	Remarks and references to Appendices
BRESLE	1.7.1916		Company moved from ST. GRATIEN to BRESLE.	
	2.		C.O., 2 Officers, 9 N.C.Os & 78 left to take up work with 1st home Counties R.E. 8th Div. in AVELUY DEFENCES.	
	3		Remainder of Coy. (dismounted) not working with 8th Div. paraded at 5 p.m. & proceeded on pontoon waggons to Engineers Pk. No. 1. according to instructions. Returned to billets on arrival of waggons to that effect.	
	4		Took over from Home Counties Field Coy R.E. 8th Div. the centre area of line formerly held by 15th Div. opposite OVILLERS. 4 Sections moved to AVELUY DEFENCES about 4 p.m. It night Coy. assisted by the 5th Northamptonshire Pioneers dug a trench across "No mans land" from junction of ARGYLL ST. & with front line to point X.13.T.96. / Pts. 154 Sections continued work on trench as on 4th & left at 8 p.m. " 273 " dug advance trench from app. 5. to SUNKEN 85.	
	5		Communication trench could be along St. Edward dumpled & resited. Trenches sandworked.	
	6		Headquarters & tool cart moved to AVELUY DEFENCES. German front line reconnoitred with a view to making strong points. Two Strong Points were arranged for, but owing to confusion in trenches carrying parties went astray.	
AVELUY DEFENCES	7			
	8		During the night sections were employed making sunken road from OVILLERS Post to old front line passable for wheeled traffic. Sections bridged footbed trenches as necessary with fuel ballast, in conjunction with Pioneers.	

Army Form C. 2118.

WAR DIARY
or
INTELLIGENCE SUMMARY.
(Erase heading not required.)

Instructions regarding War Diaries and Intelligence Summaries are contained in F. S. Regs., Part II. and the Staff Manual respectively. Title Pages will be prepared in manuscript.

Place	Date	Hour	Summary of Events and Information	Remarks and references to Appendices
VADENCOURT	9.7.1916		Work taken over by 206th Coy. R.E. of Coy. moved to VADENCOURT WOOD by Motor Lorries.	
	10. " .		Captn Rev. Darlington relinquished command of Coy. & left to take up duties as S.O. F.E. C.E. IX Corps.	
			Capt. A. Forrest Major of R.A. Ferguson took over command of Coy.	
BUS-LES-ARTOIS	11 " .		Coy. moved by road from Vadencourt to Bus-Les-Artois.	
	12 " .		Fatigues cleaning camp & wagons.	
	13 " .		" Inspection by O.C. F.E. 12 D. Div.	
	14 " .		Repairing wells. Cleaning wagon equipment.	
	15 " .		Repairs to wells completed. Wells, latrines inspected by D.S.E.	
	16 Sunday		Church parade.	
	17.7.16		Exercises & drill.	
	18		Resting & fires.	
MAILLY MAILLET	19		Company's Baricot disposal at E.H.L. & 29th Div. Marched to Mailly Mallet. Unless cancelled in evening.	
BUS-LES-ARTOIS	20.7.16		Company returned to Bus. U.L.O. 9 Two officers reported to E.H.L. & 4th Div. arrangements made for taking over section of line from Hebuterne to Colincamps	
MAILLY MAILLET	21.7.16		Left BUS-LES-ARTOIS 8 a.m. Bivouacked in huts at P.2.a.2.2. taking over work of trenches held by 56 R.F. Div. 5 Section started work on dug-out T Sect. on Fonquevillers	

1577 Wt. W10791/1773 500,000 1/15 D. D. & L. A.D.S.S./Forms/C. 2118.

Army Form C. 2118.

WAR DIARY
or
INTELLIGENCE SUMMARY.

(Erase heading not required.)

Instructions regarding War Diaries and Intelligence Summaries are contained in F. S. Regs., Part II. and the Staff Manual respectively. Title pages will be prepared in manuscript.

68th FIELD COMPANY
JUL 1916
ROYAL ENGINEERS

Place	Date	Hour	Summary of Events and Information	Remarks and references to Appendices
MAILLY MAILLET	22/7/1916		Work on Deep Dug-outs in front line trenches South. Also work on Tramway.	
	23		" " "	
	24		" " "	
BOUZINCOURT	25		Handed over to 123rd Coy. R.E. & moved to Puis-les-Artois at 9 a.m. arrived at 10.30 a.m. and left again at 5-p.m for Bouzincourt arrived at 6.20 p.m.	
	26		Reconnoitering & taking over work from 1st & 5th Field Coy R.E (T) Working on Strong Points.	
	27		" " " 4 Sections V.B. dismounted moved into Dug-outs at W.12.d.	
	28		" " "	
	29		" " "	
	30		" " "	
	31		" " "	

J. Ingomar
Capt & Adjt.
COMMANDING 68th (FIELD) COMPANY R.E.

MAJOR, R.E.
COMMANDING 68th (FIELD) COMPANY R.E.

12/69/RE Vol 12

CONFIDENTIAL.

WAR DIARY

OF

69TH FIELD COY. R.E.

FROM 31-7-16 TO 30-8-16

WAR DIARY
INTELLIGENCE SUMMARY
(Erase heading not required.)

Army Form C. 2118.

Place	Date	Hour	Summary of Events and Information	Remarks and references to Appendices
Near ANCRE N.12.A.4.2.	1 Aug 1916		Working on Strong Points near OVILLERS & POZIÈRES. During night of 31/7/16 1 Section digging out Com: trench X.3.C.1.2. to X.3.C.9.5.	
	2		Working on Strong Points & Dug-outs. 1 N.C.O. & 1 man wounded.	
	3		" " " " " " " " " 1 Sect. "standing to" at night to consolidate positions gained. 1 man killed 5 1st.	
	4		2 Sects. working " " " " " " 1 = Bomb Dug-out. 1 Sect. without trenches during attack mounted Consolidated (intermediate trench) Seized. (1 Man W/d, 1 N.C.O. W/d).	
	5		" " " " " " " (3 Sprs. W/d)	
	6		" " " " " " "	
	7		" " " " " " " 1 N.C.O. killed, 1 N.C.O. wounded.	
	8		" " " " " " " At night Lt. Keelan, Cpl. Drury + 5 Sprs. consolidating back of RATION TRENCH. After attack by Suffolks, making Bomb Blocks & M.G. emplacements.	
	9		" " " " " " " At 1 a.m. 2 Sections were relieved by 2 Sections of 10 Coy. No. 1 Section proceeding to ANCUY No. 3 Sect. to BOUZINCOURT for work under O.C. 10 Coy.	
	10		At night laying out tapes in front of RATION TRENCH. Strong Points & Dug-outs. Investigating water supply at OVILLERS. At night laying out tapes about 100 yds. in advance of the one laid out during night of 9/10. Working on 2 Saps from RATION TRENCH into no-man's-land.	
	11		Strong Points + Bomb Dug-outs. Water Supply at OVILLERS. At night taking up tapes laid during night of 9/10.	
	12		Strong Points & Dug-outs. At night consolidating Captured trench + making C.T. from Captured trench to RATION TRENCH.	

F. T. Williams Brevet
MAJOR, R.E.
COMMANDING 69th (FIELD) COMPANY R.E.

WAR DIARY
INTELLIGENCE SUMMARY.
(Erase heading not required.)

Army Form C. 2118.

Place	Date	Hour	Summary of Events and Information	Remarks and references to Appendices
BOUZINCOURT	13-8-16		Coy concentrated at Bouzincourt during afternoon.	
	14		Kit Inspections. 1 Sect. breaking huts. 19 Reinforcements received.	
			O.C. inspected mounted section and horses.	
	15		Erecting huts and fatigues.	
	16		" " "	
	17		Moved from Bouzincourt at 5.30.A.M. Dismounted by Bus. Mounted by road.	
AUTHIEULE	18		" " AUTHIEULE " " "	
LIENCOURT	19		Clean arms inspection + fatigues.	
"	20		Church Parade.	
"	21		Inspection by G.O.C.	
"	22		Moved from LIENCOURT to WARLUS in the morning.	
			Mounted Section & transport remained at Warlus. 3 Sections + H.Q. moved in afternoon	
	23		to ARRAS. No 2 Sect. moved to R.E. Park DAINVILLE	
ARRAS			Clean arms inspection + fatigue. Taking over from 69th Field Coy. R.E.	
	24		Working into 68th Coy.	
	25		Completed taking over work in H Sector + R.E. Park.	
	26		Working with 35th Bde. Employed on Dug-outs, M.G. Emb., Stokes S. Emb., Morter Emb.,	
	27		" " " " " " " " " " "	
	31		& Renovation of H.B. Fire, Ronville Keep.	

69th FIELD COMPANY
Date August
ROYAL ENGINEERS

MAJOR, R.E.
COMMANDING 69th (FIELD) COMPANY R.E.

Vol 13

<u>CONFIDENTIAL</u>

<u>WAR</u> <u>DIARY</u>

OF

<u>69TH FIELD COY.</u>

<u>ROYAL</u> <u>ENGINEERS</u>

FROM 30-8-16 TO 29-9-16

Army Form C. 2118.

WAR DIARY
INTELLIGENCE SUMMARY.
(Erase heading not required.)

Instructions regarding War Diaries and Intelligence Summaries are contained in F. S. Regs., Part II. and the Staff Manual respectively. Title pages will be prepared in manuscript.

Place	Date	Hour	Summary of Events and Information	Remarks and references to Appendices
ARRAS	1.9.1916 to 26.9.1916		Mounted Section & Transport (less Pontoon Wagons) at BERNEVILLE. No. 2 Section at R.E. Park DAINVILLE. 3 Sections working on Deep Dug-outs, M.G. emplacements, Stokes Gun emplacements, Mortar emplacements, Ronville Reserves, Secret Keep, Achicourt Keep and Gas-frame emplacements in H. Sector.	
	27		Handed over to 89th Field Coy. R.E.	
	28		Night at 21/28. Dismounted portion left ARRAS for bus for MILLY. Mounted portion by road during the night via WARLUS to MILLY.	
MILLY	29		MILLY to VILLERS-BOCAGE " " " Villers to BECORDEL near ALBERT	
	30		Dismounted portion by bus & marching from MILLY to BECORDEL.	

E. Nixon Major, R.E.
Commanding 59th Field Company R.E.

vol 14.

War Diary

69th Field Company.

Royal Engineers

for

Month

ending 31st October.

Army Form C. 2118.

WAR DIARY
INTELLIGENCE SUMMARY.
(Erase heading not required.)

Instructions regarding War Diaries and Intelligence Summaries are contained in F. S. Regs., Part II. and the Staff Manual respectively. Title pages will be prepared in manuscript.

Place	Date	Hour	Summary of Events and Information	Remarks and references to Appendices
POMMIERS.	1.10.1916.		Moved from BECORDEL - BECOURT to POMMIERS BECOURT at 62c.N.W.A.1.6.4.	
LONGUEVAL	2.10.1916.	"	POMMIERS to Hutments at West LONGUEVAL at 57c.S.W. S.23.a.4.7.	
	3/5 "	"	Took over from 126th Field Coy. R.E.	
	6 "	"	Working on COCOA LANE & GAS ALLEY north of DELVILLE WOOD.	
	7 "	"	" " " " " " " " "	2 ½ " Tripshells 91 off Flannelette
	8/11 "	"	FLAKE ALLEY & making road from LONGUEVAL to FLERS.	" " " " "
	12 "	"	" " " " " " " " "	" " " " "
	13 "	"	" " " " " " " " "	" " Erecting screens.
	14/19 "	"	Making road from LONGUEVAL to FLERS.	
	"	"	" " " " " " " " "	3 Men Killed 9 " wounded.
	"	"	" " " " " " " " "	& making Bangalore Torpedoes.
FRICOURT	20 "	"	Moved to Billets in NISSON HUTS. at 62c.W.E. F.18.a.	
	2/29 "	"	Working under C.R.E. XV Corps Troops erecting Nisson Huts and other accommodation for a Brigade Camp.	
DERNAN-COURT	30.		Moved from FRICOURT to DERNANCOURT.	
TALMAS.	31.		Transport moved from DERNANCOURT to TALMAS.	

F. Ingram
MAJOR, R.E.
COMMANDING 69th (FIELD) COMPANY R.E.

CONFIDENTIAL

WAR DIARY
NOVEMBER 1916.

69th Field Coy R.E.

Army Form C. 2118.

WAR DIARY
or
INTELLIGENCE SUMMARY.
(Erase heading not required.)

Instructions regarding War Diaries and Intelligence Summaries are contained in F. S. Regs., Part II. and the Staff Manual respectively. Title pages will be prepared in manuscript.

Place	Date	Hour	Summary of Events and Information	Remarks and references to Appendices
Pon TOULLENS	1.11.1916.		Mounted portion moved from THOMAS to TOULLENS. By road.	
			Dismounted " " DERNANCOURT to GOUY by bus.	
			" " " TOULLENS to GOUY by bus.	
GOUY	2.11.		Mounted " " TOULLENS to GOUY by road.	
"	3.11.		Drills Fatigues & Inoculation.	
ARRAS	5		Mounted portion moved to ARRAS.	
			No. 3. Section to R.E. Park MAINVILLE.	
			H.Q. Nos 1, 2 & 3 Sections dismounted to ARRAS. Took over work in H. Sector from the 89 & 4 Field Coys R.E.	
ARRAS	6/30		Working in H. Sector with 25th Inf. Bde, on Dug-outs, Shelters, Wire Entanglements, Trench Works Lamps, Trench Mortar Slides, O.P.s, Patrol Lines, Steps, Toeville Defences, Achicourt Defences, Toeville Sump Road Line, Trench Tramway, and also finishing Incinerators & various odd jobs in ARRAS.	

E. Tyack
Lieut R.E.
for O.C. COMMANDING 69th (FIELD) COMPANY R.E.

WAR DIARY
INTELLIGENCE SUMMARY

Army Form C. 2118.

Vol 16

Place	Date	Hour	Summary of Events and Information	Remarks and references to Appendices
ARRAS	1.12.1916. to 16.12.1916.		Working in H. Sector with 35th & 9th Divs on Reg¹ Dug-outs, Machine Gun Emplacements, Trench Mortar Emplacements & Stores, Bench & Sawmill, Achicourt Reserves, O.Ps. RONVILLE Reserves, RONVILLE Gun-Pits & c. also Military Incinerators and various other jobs in ARRAS. 1 Section employed in R.E. Park THINVILLE.	51st Div 4000 G.27.E. 51st Div 4000 J.21.E.
DUISANS.	17.		Transport moved from WARLUS to DUISANS.	
			No. 3. Sect. " " THINVILLE " "	
			Rmd. of Coy " " ARRAS " "	
LIGNEREUIL.	18.		Coy. moved from DUISANS to LIGNEREUIL by road.	51st Div 4000 J.21.E.
	19.		Physical Drill & Fatigues.	
	20.		Kit Inspection. Cleaning equipment. Rifle Drills & Exercises.	
	21st 22nd 23rd		Training.	
	24.		Sunday. Church Parades.	
	25.		Christmas Day.	
	26. 27. 28.		Training.	
	29.		Instruction by C.R.E.	
	30.		" " of Rifle Demonstration & Model Men. Cleaning horse lines.	
	31.		Sunday. Fatigues.	

E.Ryan. Capt. R.E.
Commanding 69th (FIELD) COMPANY R.E.

CONFIDENTIAL.

WAR DIARY

OF

69TH. FIELD COY., R.E

From 1-1-17 To 31-1-17

WAR DIARY
INTELLIGENCE SUMMARY.
(Erase heading not required.)

Army Form C. 2118.

Place	Date	Hour	Summary of Events and Information	Remarks and references to Appendices
LIGNEREUIL	1.1.1917.		Marching Order inspection by O.C.	S.F.d 21.E.11
	2		" " " C.R.E.	
	3/6		Training	
	7		Sunday. Church Parade	
	8/9		Training	
	10/13		Working on Practice trenches in training area.	
	14		No. 3. Section proceeded to HOUVIN & Nº 4 Section to LIENCOURT repairing huts. Remainder of Coy. working on Practice trenches, making notice boards, horse standings &c.
	15/27		As on the 14th	
	28		Sunday. Gas helmet inspection & Church parade	
	29		As on the 14th	
	30		" " " "	
	31		" " " " No. 3 Section returned from Houvin.	

a/ [signature] Lieut R.E.
Commanding 98th (Field) Company R.E.

Confidential

Vol 18

War Diary

12 Div

of

69th Field Coy. R.E.

From 1.2.1917 to 28.2.1917

(Volume 21)

Army Form C. 2118.

WAR DIARY or INTELLIGENCE SUMMARY.

(Erase heading not required.)

Instructions regarding War Diaries and Intelligence Summaries are contained in F.S. Regs., Part II. and the Staff Manual respectively. Title pages will be prepared in manuscript.

Place	Date	Hour	Summary of Events and Information	Remarks and references to Appendices
LIGNEREUIL	1.2.1917		No 1 Section working on Practice trenches in Training Area.	
	2		" " " " " " " " " " " " " " " " " Ducking at VIENCOURT.	
	3		Nos 2 & 3 ... proceeded to ARRAS to relieve 2 Section of 204th Field Coy working on Artillery preparation under C.E. VI Corps.	
	4		1.N.C.O & 8 Men working under C.R.E. in LE CAUROY Woods.	
	5		" " " " " Sawmills at FERVENT	
	6		As on 1st	
ARRAS	7/22		2nd " " 1 N.C.O & 7 Men attached to C.R.E. & told off into.	
			3rd " Major W. Hyde Kelly. D.S.O. R.E. took over command of Coy.	
			No 4 Section to work with Nos 2 & 3 Sections. Remainder as on 4th.	
			O.C. & Coy Office moved to ARRAS. Remainder as on 5th.	
			3 Sections working on Artillery preparation under VI Corps.	
			Detachments at LE CAUROY. FERVENT + C.R.E. as on 3rd.	
			Remainder L No 1 Sect. on practice trenches in Training Area.	
	23/28		S.H. transport + Coy Capt. at LIGNEREUIL	
			3 Sections at ARRAS. working on Trench Mortar Emplacements under 12th Div. T.M.O.	
			Remainder of Coy as on 7th & 6 22.	

W. Hyde Kelly.
MAJOR, R.E.
COMMANDING 68th (FIELD) COMPANY R.E.

1577 Wt. W10791/1773 500,000 1/15 D. D. & L. A.D.S.S./Forms/C. 2118.

Vol 19

Confidential

War Diary
of
69th Field Coy. R.E.
From 1.5.17 To 31.5.17

(Volume 22)

Army Form C. 2118.

WAR DIARY
INTELLIGENCE SUMMARY.
(Erase heading not required.)

Instructions regarding War Diaries and Intelligence Summaries are contained in F. S. Regs., Part II. and the Staff Manual respectively. Title pages will be prepared in manuscript.

Place	Date	Hour	Summary of Events and Information	Remarks and references to Appendices
ARRAS.	1. March 1917 to 19th March 1917		3 Sections at ARRAS working on French Mortar Emplacements, Dug-outs, Tramlines &c under 12th Div. F.M.O. No. 1 Section at LIGNEREUIL on practice trenches Detachment at LE CAUROY Roads Cutting Trees. ,, ,, PREVENT Sawmills. Captain & H.Q. Transport at LIGNEREUIL.	
	20		No. 1 Sect at LIGNEREUIL and detachment at LE CAUROY moved to ARRAS and took up work with the 3 Sections on 21st. Remainder as on 19th.	
	21nd 22nd		Coy. Capt & H.Q. Transport at LIGNEREUIL. Detachments at PREVENT and LE CAUROY 4 Sections less one detachment on Artillery preparations on 20th.	
	23.		Coy. Capt & H.Q. Transport moved from LIGNEREUIL to AGNEZ les DUISANS. Remainder as on 22nd.	
	24. 3.17.		Coy. Capt & H.Q. Transport at AGNEZ les DUISANS. Detachment at PREVENT Sawmill ,, ,, T.S. & R.E. Yard depots. O.C. Coy. 7.S. with 4 Sections at ARRAS working on Artillery preparations as on the 20th.	

W. Kerby
MAJOR, R.E.
COMMANDING 60th (FIELD) COMPANY R.E.

Confidential

Vol 20

War Diary
of
69th Field Coy. R.E.

From 1.4.1917 To 30.4.1917

(Volume 23)

Army Form C. 2118.

WAR DIARY
INTELLIGENCE SUMMARY.
(Erase heading not required.)

Place	Date	Hour	Summary of Events and Information	Remarks and references to Appendices
ARRAS.	1.4.1917.		Coy. Captain & H.S. transfered to AGNEZ-les-DUISANS. Detachment at FREVENT Sawmill.	
	2nd		C.H.E. & T.O. for odd jobs.	
	3rd		O.C., Coy. H.S. with 4 Sections to ARRAS working on artillery preparations.	
			Ditto. Detachment rejoined from C.H.E.	
	4th		Coy. ceased work on artillery preparations at 12 - noon and moved into cellars.	
			Standing to in cellars. Arranging details for operations. Officers & N.C.O's survey's etc.	
	5th		Ds on H & V Day	
	6th		" " W "	
	7th		" " X "	
	8th		" " Y " Easter Sunday. Church Service	
	9th		Z Day. Coy. moved off for the offensive as ordered under 15th Div. Nos. 1 & 3 Sections worked with R.E. Battalion under Lt. Sandeman Tit & for construction of Strong Points at FEUCHY CHAPEL. No. 2. Section worked with Menzies to build dummy Gun Emplacements ARRAS towards FEUCHY CHAPEL.	

WAR DIARY

INTELLIGENCE SUMMARY.

(Erase heading not required.)

Army Form C. 2118.

Place	Date	Hour	Summary of Events and Information	Remarks and references to Appendices
ARRAS	9th.4.17 4th		No. 4 Section under 2/Lt Eaton divided: 1 N.C.O. L/Cpl Pleas and 6 attached infantry travelling German front trenches, remainder of section making track and road across German trenches. At 6.-a.m. The sections moved off to Q's assembly place via cellars and tunnel. The attack progressed according to programme. No. 2 Section was ordered to East Dainsley by 12.- noon. Track horse track started about same time. 2/Lt Eaton's party started travelling German trenches as soon as Black system infantry. It carried on this work until "Blue line" (second system) had been captured (and then returned to cellars in ARRAS at about 4.- a.m. on 10th inst. Remainder of No. 4 Section on Yack Horse track worked until midnight and carried line as far as Yas as OBSERVATION RIDGE. No. 2 Section worked in conjunction with 5th Northampton Pioneers (Sappers forming baits while a Coy. of Pioneers (5th Northampton 2nd Re/Regt) made the formation (tamels). Nos. 1 & 3 Sections remained in their cellars all day as FEUCHY CHAPEL was not completely taken. 1/Lt Tabbit started with 4 Sappers for special demolition and fire extinguishing	

WAR DIARY
INTELLIGENCE SUMMARY

(Erase heading not required.)

Army Form C. 2118.

Place	Date	Hour	Summary of Events and Information	Remarks and references to Appendices
ARRAS.	10.4.1917.		Nos. 2 & 4 Sections continued their work as on the 9th. Nos. 1 & 3 " rolled out at 1 - p.m. to take on employment of carttrack. Impeded by traffic. 3 Coys. 5th Northants Pioneers placed at O.C.'s disposal for same work. Old Sections returned to billets in Arras at/as 6pm. night.	
	11.4.1917.		Nos. 2 & 4 Sections continued their work " 1 & 3 " " " About 10 a.m. orders were received to return the 100 Infantry attached for work to their Battalions. About 11 a.m. orders were received at HdQrs. for whole Coy. to move into cellars in the Gustav Colin, ARRAS. More men employed, when further orders came for Coy. to go up to FEUCHY CHAPEL for consolidation work under G.O.C. 35th Inf. Brigade. Coy. collected and marched off at 6 - p.m. with tool carts & forage carts. (great block of traffic on main road.) O.C. went ahead and obtained instructions from the Brigadier. Sappers brought forward with picks & shovels while tool carts were left to follow in the stream of traffic. "ARISON ROUGE" about 9 - P.M. and went straight Sections reached "Coy. H.Qrs." arriving German support line to front line, joining 69th Field Coy. R.E.	

1577 Wt.W10791/1773 500,000 4/15 D&D.&L. A.D.S.S./Forms/C 2118.

Army Form C. 2118.

WAR DIARY
INTELLIGENCE SUMMARY.
(Erase heading not required.)

Instructions regarding War Diaries and Intelligence Summaries are contained in F.S. Regs., Part II. and the Staff Manual respectively. Title pages will be prepared in manuscript.

Place	Date	Hour	Summary of Events and Information	Remarks and references to Appendices
Neuville-Capel.	12.4.1917		The night of 11/12th was very cold, snow squalls at frequent intervals. There was no accommodation at MAISON ROUGE which did not exist. The sections worked until 4 a.m. when they returned to the Tool Cart at MAISON ROUGE and waited for daylight. Some 500-600 yds of trench had been reversed. Company arrived. Further orders on that side. I endeavoured to make shelters in the bank of the road. About 3 p.m. orders from Brigade were received to stand by ready for return to billets in ARRAS on relief of the Division. O.C. with 1 N.C.O. reconnoitred positions for strong points on ORANGE and CHAPEL Hills and reported to Brigadier. Company marched back to billets in ARRAS about 9 p.m.	
ARRAS	13.4.1917		Rest day in ARRAS. Detachment returned from FREVENT.	
"	14		Fatigues. Cleaning Equipment & Wagons. Inspection by O.C.	
"	15th /24th		Working under C.E. VI Corps. repairing roads, hewing up Dud Shells, salving R.E. Materials, erecting Church Army Tents, and various odd jobs.	

Army Form C. 2118.

WAR DIARY
or
INTELLIGENCE SUMMARY.

(Erase heading not required.)

Instructions regarding War Diaries and Intelligence Summaries are contained in F. S. Regs., Part II. and the Staff Manual respectively. Title pages will be prepared in manuscript.

Place	Date	Hour	Summary of Events and Information	Remarks and references to Appendices
FEUCHY	25.4.1917		Sections moved from ARRAS 5-a.m. to relieve 93rd & 78th Field Coys in the front line. Move to collars at FEUCHY completed by 5-7. p.m. Companys turned out for work on line of Strong Points on Capt Lane & Yorkshire Front Lat 7. to Yule Parties delayed en route by shelling and reached their work by 11-PM and worked till 4-am when it became time to return before daylight. Work done. Wiring 8 Strong Points. No Casts. 17th Field C. taken with 15 O.R.s and men laid out new Support trench with infantry working parties. Casualties 1. Wounded.	
	26.4.1917		Company paraded for work 8-P.M. with carrying of 100 Essex Work done: Fencing up & wiring Strong Points with double wire stakes Strengthened existing wiring and put up 2 new obstacles on neck of land on Chapel trench to secure Machine Gun Post. Also deepened Fire trench to 4 feet. Casualties 1 Killed 2 Wounded.	
	27.4.1917		Coy. ordered to take part in operations for morning of 28th	

WAR DIARY
or
INTELLIGENCE SUMMARY

Army Form C. 2118.

Place	Date	Hour	Summary of Events and Information	Remarks and references to Appendices
FEUCHY	28.4.1917		Left Billets at 1- A.M. Each Section had 1 Platoon of Pioneers of "L" Coy 5 Northamptonshire Regt. Reached their assembly place with material at 3- a.m. Attack took place at 4.25" Sections not successful in reaching objectives. Sections remained in their trenches all day rendering assistance in repairing damaged trenches and at nightfall when they proceeded to wire the front line and make a strong point. Casualties 11 wounded. Coy. returned to Fields 5.30 a.m.	
	29.		Coy. rest out for work on consolidation together with Pioneers as on the 28th. Work done: Wiring front line and making another Strong Point. Also clearing beyond trench which had been much knocked about. Casualties 4 O.R. wounded. 2 O.R. Killed. 1 Officer Wounded	
	30		Coy. returned, relieved by 70 & 97th Field Coys and moved back to Dugouts at Railway Triangle 6 - P.M. H. 19. B.5.8. Weather during operations 28/30th June easy.	W. Johns Kells Major RE

1577 Wt.W10791/1773 500,000 1/15 D.D.&L. A.D.S.S./Forms/C. 2118.

Confidential

№ 21

War Diary
of
69th Field Coy. R.E.

From 1.5.17 To 31.5.17

(Volume 24)

Army Form C. 2118.

WAR DIARY
INTELLIGENCE SUMMARY.
(Erase heading not required.)

Instructions regarding War Diaries and Intelligence Summaries are contained in F.S. Regs., Part II. and the Staff Manual respectively. Title pages will be prepared in manuscript.

Place	Date	Hour	Summary of Events and Information	Remarks and references to Appendices
RAILWAY TRIANGLE	May 1917 1 2 3 4		O.C. with 4 Sections at RAILWAY TRIANGLE (a) 8 Carpenters & 2 Sappers at IVORY DUMP (a) Staff with transport at ARRAS. As on the 3rd. 2 Sections allowing entrances to R. Dug outs at Railway Triangle, and removing trees from SCARPE CANAL. 2 Sections working under O.C. 87th Field Coy on communication trench from I.31.C.7. to I.31.C.7.4. to I.31.H.4.9.3. 1 Spr mortally wounded. No sights at ARCH S.	Sheet 51B H19.c.5.7.
	5 & 6" 7"		As on the 4th. 2 Sections working on CURB TRENCH I.31.C.4.5. to I.31.C.8.6. & 2 Sections on ELBOW Trench Casualties. 1 Sergt Killed 9 O.R. wounded. 1 Wounded German taken prisoner in a shell hole by Lt Sandeman while laying new line.	
	8		During night of 7/8 making ELBOW trench. Work delayed for 1½ hours on account of enemy shrapnel shelling. 1 O.R. slightly wounded.	
	9 10		Work during night of 8/9 & 9/10 on BB & 1 Sergt & 2 O.R. wounded. " " 9/10 & 10/11. New communication trench from BAYONET to RIFLE trenches (H.36.d.9.6 to I.31.a.7.7 and I.31.a.7 finding 2 feet deep throughout 600 yds	
	11 12		Work during night of 10/11 as on 9/10 & 5 feet " " 11/12 CURRY LANE cleared to a depth of 5'.6" (150 yds)	

N. Sgr Kerr

Army Form C. 2118.

WAR DIARY
INTELLIGENCE SUMMARY.
(Erase heading not required.)

Instructions regarding War Diaries and Intelligence Summaries are contained in F. S. Regs., Part II. and the Staff Manual respectively. Title pages will be prepared in manuscript.

Place	Date	Hour	Summary of Events and Information	Remarks and references to Appendices
RAILWAY TRIANGLE	14.5.1917		4 Sections with 200 Infantry Reconstructed 450 yds of T.S.16 Plays with fire steps in ORANGE LINE during night of 13/14.	
	15		During night of 14/15 120 yds of trench Reconstructed & 100 yds trench cleared in ORANGE LINE. New C.T. from ORANGE LINE to H.23.d.5.8. dug through, to average depth of 3ft 9450 yds of existing C.T. widened to 3ft.	
ARRAS.	16		During night of 15/16 RAILWAY C.T. deepened to 5'. At 6. a.m. the front half of 2nd Lt. Ford bus was damaged by shell fire. The shell set alight to the car & burnt out the front half. The seat half was saturated in contents but still safe. by Sergt Ruffingall with the aid of L/C N Jackson & Spr Yates.  O.C. & 4 Sections moved to Billets in Arras.	(2) Sheet SIC
	17		Inspection by O.C.	
	18		Preparing for move.	
SIMENCOURT	19		Coy. moved to SIMENCOURT. (4)	(4) Sheet SIC 9.10 & 3.2
	20		Guard House. Shoe & SB drawn from Div & Park Store & issued.	
	21		Rifle exercises & talks	
	22		" "	
	23		G.O.C. presented the Military Medal Ribbon to 4 NCOs & 1 Spr. and inspected the Coy.	

Army Form C. 2118.

WAR DIARY
INTELLIGENCE SUMMARY.
(Erase heading not required.)

Instructions regarding War Diaries and Intelligence Summaries are contained in F. S. Regs., Part II. and the Staff Manual respectively. Title pages will be prepared in manuscript.

Place	Date	Hour	Summary of Events and Information	Remarks and references to Appendices
IVERGNY	24.5.1917		Company moved from SINCOURT to IVERGNY (C) Dismounted by bus. Transport & cyclists by road.	(C) Sheet 51C N 21.d.2.0
	25		Squad drill, Physical drill & recreation. 42 Reinforcement received	
	26		" " "	
	27		Sunday. Rest day.	
	28		Squad drill, Physical drill & recreation	
	29		Coy. Athletic Sports commenced 7.30 a.m. 5 Reinforcements arrived	
	30		" " " "	
	31		Physical Exercises & training for Coy. Sports.	

D. Style Kelly.
MAJOR, R.E.
COMMANDING 69th (FIELD) COMPANY R.E.

Confidential

Vol 22

War Diary
of
69th Field Coy. RE

From 1.6.17
to 30.6.17

(Volume 25)

Army Form C. 2118.

WAR DIARY
INTELLIGENCE SUMMARY.
(Erase heading not required.)

Instructions regarding War Diaries and Intelligence Summaries are contained in F.S. Regs., Part II. and the Staff Manual respectively. Title pages will be prepared in manuscript.

Place	Date	Hour	Summary of Events and Information	Remarks and references to Appendices
IVERGNY	1 June 17		Company at IVERGNY in Rest Bev. Drill & R.E. Sports	Maj. S/C
N21d.5.2	2		Drills. Coy concert in the evening	
	3		Sunday. Church Parade	
	4		Drill. Cleaning equipment & Lecture by O.C. to NCOs	
	5		Marching Order Parade. Divisional Sports	
	6		" " and inspection by C.R.E.	
	7		Rifle exercises, London & Field D.S.E., Feints & lashings Musketry courses	
	8		Moving as on the 7th. Gymnm: Coy attended Bde Sports.	
	9		Fatigues & Training.	
	10		Sunday	
	11		Drills & demolitions. Small Box Respirators inspected by Gas Officer.	
	12		Baths & Training.	
	13		Harness inspection. Visiting by O.C. & Drills	
	14		Physical Drill & Musketry	
	15		Physical, Squad & Musketry Drill. G.O.C. 12th Div: inspected Coy whilst about to supply reinforcements returned to R.S.R.E. Reinforcements Coy.	
	16		G.O.C. 12th Div. presented Military Medal Ribbons to L/CSM. Jackson & Spr. Cole Physical & Squad Drill	

L. Hyde Kelly,
MAJOR, R.E.
COMMANDING 69th (FIELD) COMPANY R.E.

Army Form C. 2118.

WAR DIARY
INTELLIGENCE SUMMARY.
(Erase heading not required.)

Instructions regarding War Diaries and Intelligence Summaries are contained in F. S. Regs., Part II. and the Staff Manual respectively. Title pages will be prepared in manuscript.

Place	Date	Hour	Summary of Events and Information	Remarks and references to Appendices
ARRAS.	17th June 17		Company moved in motor lorries from IVERGNY to ARRAS. Move completed by 8 P.M. Very successful.	MAP 51b
Nr. TILLOY	18		Dismounted section moved to bivouacs near TILLOY H.32.a.8.2.	H.36
	19 to 30		Working on new C.H.E. 12th Div. on Dugouts, Strong Points, Hill Post, Observation Post, Tracks, Communication Trench, New Support Trench, SNAFFLE Trench, & ORANGE LANE.	T.31 } 51b N.3

L. Van Keer
MAJOR, R.E.
COMMANDING 88th (FIELD) COMPANY R.E.

Confidential

Vol 23

War Diary

of

69th Field Coy R.E.

From 1/7/17 to 31/7/17

Volume (26)

Army Form C. 2118.

WAR DIARY
or
INTELLIGENCE SUMMARY.
(Erase heading not required.)

Instructions regarding War Diaries and Intelligence Summaries are contained in F.S. Regs., Part II. and the Staff Manual respectively. Title pages will be prepared in manuscript.

Place	Date	Hour	Summary of Events and Information	Remarks and references to Appendices
51.N.W.6.c.1. Pont Tilloy	1. July 1917 to 31. 7. 17.		Working under C.R.E. 12th Division, on making & repairing Communication Trenches: BRIDOON LANE, ORANGE LANE, NEW RANGE LANE, ORCHARD SUPPORT and CORPS LINE. Also taking out new benches.	
			Casualties: 7.7. 1.O.R. Wounded 14.7. 5.O.R. Wounded 16.7. 1.O.R. Wounded. 20.7. 11th PARDUS Killed 2.O.R. Wounded.	
			Transport at HONVILLE. Ration Wagons used daily for transporting R.E. Materials to forward dumps.	
	16.7.17.		Major W.H. Kelly R.S.C. R.E. relinquished command of Company to take up appointment of C.R.E. 58th Division	
	17.		Major M.J. Ferguson 14. E assumed command of Company	

J. Ferguson
MAJOR. R.E.
COMMANDING 69th (FIELD) COMPANY R.E.

Confidential

No 24

War Diary
of
69th Field Coy. R.E.

From 1.8.17 To 31.8.17

(Volume 27)

Army Form C. 2118.

WAR DIARY

INTELLIGENCE SUMMARY.
(Erase heading not required.)

Place	Date	Hour	Summary of Events and Information	Remarks and references to Appendices
Mh TILLOY N.2.d.5.7.	1 Aug 1917		Working under C.R.E. on Communication Trenches ORCHARD RESERVE	Appx. 51B
	4 to 20	17th		
	18/20		As on 17th. Also on SWORD LANE	
	21st to 31st		Ditto on C.Ts ORCHARD RESERVE, SWORD LANE & EAST RESERVE. Making a concrete O.P. in MONCHY. No battle casualties during the month.	

J. Taylor
MAJOR, R.E.
COMMANDING 69th (FIELD) COMPANY R.E.

Duponto

CONFIDENTIAL

WAR DIARY

OF

69ᵀᴴ FIELD COMPANY. R.E.

From 31.8.17.　　　　　**To** 29.9.17.

Army Form C. 2118.

WAR DIARY
or
INTELLIGENCE SUMMARY.
(Erase heading not required.)

Instructions regarding War Diaries and Intelligence Summaries are contained in F. S. Regs., Part II. and the Staff Manual respectively. Title pages will be prepared in manuscript.

Place	Date	Hour	Summary of Events and Information	Remarks and references to Appendices
Nex TILLOY N.3.d.5.9.	1.9.1917 to 30.9.1917		Working on O.P. in MONCHY. Making SECRET TRENCH N 7's. EAST RESERVE, ORCHARD RESERVE, CANNISTER ST, CIRCLE TRENCH, and SWORD LANE, repairs. " " Making new trench at N.6.d.9.9. " " Aid Post in CIRCLE TRENCH. " " Burying Cable.	

E.Ryan Capt R.E.
Commanding 69th (Field Company) R.E.

WAR DIARY

Army Form C. 2118.

INTELLIGENCE SUMMARY.
(Erase heading not required.)

Instructions regarding War Diaries and Intelligence Summaries are contained in F.S. Regs., Part II. and the Staff Manual respectively. Title pages will be prepared in manuscript.

Vol 26

Place	Date	Hour	Summary of Events and Information	Remarks and references to Appendices
Near TILLOY N.2.d.5.4.	1.10.1917		Working under R.W.E. 12th Div. on O.P. at O.1.c.65.85. and trench to same. Improvements to and maintenance of EAST RESERVE, ORCHARD RESERVE, CIRCLE and Pick trenches. Erecting old Post in CIRCLE and erecting Shelters in FORE RESERVE.	51/B.
	to		Making O.P. at Cor. H⁰ 68t in CIRCLE Road. Concrete Dugout at N.2.3.10. Dug-out chamber at FEUCHY CHAPEL QUARRY. Fixing Gas Frames.	
	7.10.17		5 men working at Dist R.E. Dump	
			,, ,, ,, on shelters in Brown line	
			,, ,, ,, on gas water pipe line	
	8/10.17		As on 1st and numbering of dug outs	
	9		" 8th and new fire trench of CANISTER	
	10		" 10th and fixing sentry boxes in EAST & ORCHARD RESERVE	
	11		" 11th and erecting direction boards for string parties	
	12		" 12th and making baths & new Monchy Dump to Circle Bench	
	13		N.H. Section moved to AGNEZ-les-DUISANS for working on training camps	
	14/16		Work as on 13th	
	17/20		" " " 13th " and Gum Boot Store at O.1.c.25. Commenced O.P. at O.1.a.70.05	
	21		" " " 17th and handing over work to 526th Field Coy. R.E.	

Casualties :- 10 O.R Killed 28 Fy 1 O.R Wounded on Aug 15th

J. Wagner Major, R.E.
COMMANDING 68th (FIELD) COMPANY R.E.

Army Form C. 2118.

WAR DIARY
INTELLIGENCE SUMMARY.
(Erase heading not required.)

Place	Date	Hour	Summary of Events and Information	Remarks and references to Appendices
HAUTEVILLE	22.10.17		Offr Ranking over to 526th Fld Coy R.E. the H.Q. & 3 sections moved to HAUTEVILLE.	51.C
GD RULLECOURT	25.		Coy. marched to GRANDE RULLECOURT.	
	26		Cleaning equipment and fatigues. Nos. 2 & 3 sections moved to 20 E Div Area (Mounted by road 9 dismounted by rail.)	
	27		Cleaning equipment & fatigues. Coy. H.Q. & No.1. Section marched to HEBRUVE.	
REBREUVE	28		" " " " " " " " "	
BLANGERMONT	29		No.4. Section rejoined " BLANGERMONT.	
	30		Cleaning equipment & improving billets.	
	31			

Signed
MAJOR, R.E.
COMMANDING 69th (FIELD) COMPANY R.E.

Vol 27

CONFIDENTIAL.

WAR DIARY.

OF

69TH FIELD COY. R.E.

From 1.11.17   To 29.11.17

(VOLUME 30.)

Army Form C. 2118.

WAR DIARY
or
INTELLIGENCE SUMMARY.
(Erase heading not required.)

Place	Date	Hour	Summary of Events and Information	Remarks and references to Appendices
BLANGERMONT	1.11.17		H.Q. & 2 Section with 12th Division in Training Area.	
"	2.11.17		Nos 2 & 3 Section at HEUDICOURT (26th Division Area).	
"	3/10.11.17		No 1 Section moved to HUMIERES for work under Div. H.Q., erecting obstacles for tanks & marking out practice trenches.	
"	11.11.17		Do on 2nd.	
"	12.11.17		No 1 Section rejoined H.Q. at BLANGERMONT from HUMIERES	
"	13.11.17		Do on 11th	
"	14.11.17		All Surplus Kit sent to Divl Kit Store at FREVENT.	
"	15.11.17		Transport & Cyclists moved off by road to HEUDICOURT	
"			Dismounted preparing to move.	
MOISLAINS	16.11.17		Dismounted Left BLANGERMONT at 4 a.m. & entrained at FREVENT & detrained at PERONNE & marched to MOISLAINS where transport found in the evening	
HEUDICOURT	17.11.17		Transport & Dismounted paraded at 4.50 p.m. & arrived at HEUDICOURT at 11 p.m.	
"	"		Transport remained at HEUDICOURT. H.Q. & Dismounted went into Dugouts at a camp 1 mile East of HEUDICOURT, where Nos 2 & 3 Section rejoined.	
"	18th		Preparing to move forward. Officers & N.C.O's reconnoitring routes and work to be done in event of an advance	
"	19.11.17			

F. Ingram
MAJOR, R.E.
COMMANDING 69th (FIELD) COMPANY R.E.

Army Form C. 2118.

WAR DIARY
or
INTELLIGENCE SUMMARY.

(Erase heading not required.)

Place	Date	Hour	Summary of Events and Information	Remarks and references to Appendices
VILLERS-GUISLAIN.	20.11.17		4 Section marched to the previously selected cellars in VILLERS-GUISLAIN, where they remained until ordered out by the Brigade at 3 A.M. On the Objective being captured, a Section joined each Battalion & assisted in the consolidation of the captured positions.	
	21.11.17 22 nd &		4 Section returned to Billets at Coy. H.Q. about 9 P.M. (No casualties).	
	23.11.17		Consolidating new positions. Fire stepping, erecting Strongpoints & Wiring	
	24.11.17		CASUALTIES Sapper Banks – Wounded –	
	25.11.17		" Larkin "	
	26.11.17		LIEUT. E.P.D. CATOR "	

Signature
MAJOR, R.E.
COMMANDING 69th (FIELD) COMPANY R.E.

CONFIDENTIAL

WAR DIARY

OF

69TH FIELD COY R.E.

FROM 29·11·17 TO 31·12·17

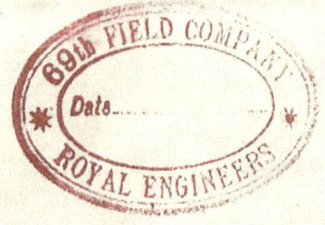

WAR DIARY or INTELLIGENCE SUMMARY

Army Form C. 2118.

Place	Date	Hour	Summary of Events and Information	Remarks and references to Appendices
HEUDICOURT	30.11.17.		On the morning of 30.11.17. the dismounted portion of the Coy. was in billets in VILLERS-GUISLAIN (Map ref. X.2.f.6.3). At about 4.a.m. the enemy put a heavy barrage on CEMETERY ROAD whereupon the Company immediately stood to in fighting order. As the barrage had lifted the enemy was seen to be advancing towards the billets from a N.E. direction. Nos. 1 & 2 sections under Lieut. Stubbings extended along Cemetery Road from X.3.C.0.0 to X.3.C.5.4. and Nos. 3 & 4 sections under Lieut. Sandeman extended across twenty fine Avenue. Both parties were compelled to retire owing to the enemy advancing on their flanks. They took up a position immediately west of GOUZEAUCOURT ROAD. This flank was again turned and they again had to give up about 200 yards of ground. On this occasion they occupied a well dug trench. This position is giving way of Division recovered 100 yds. x Dowes at a time was carried on until our lines were relieved, on which occasion being ordered on account of strong enemy pressure on the flanks. Ammunition then began to run short and the number of men was small compared to the strength of the enemy. Consequently no further offensive position was taken and the men retired in good order to about 500 yards easterly Fere Thorny, where a battalion of the Division passed through the Coy. and endeavoured to meet the advancing enemy. The men of the Company were [afterwards] at Box Dumps and marched down to the loose lines in HEUDICOURT. *Where billets [illeg.]* Their ^kink a tire was being made at REVELON PATCH.	

Army Form C. 2118.

WAR DIARY
INTELLIGENCE SUMMARY.
(Erase heading not required.)

Place	Date	Hour	Summary of Events and Information	Remarks and references to Appendices
Heudicourt	30.11.1917 (cont.)		10000 N.R. Gaston proceeded to NEVEZON FARM and garrisoned a trench about 500 yards N.E. of the Farm on South side of GONNELIEUCOURT and one of the groups of two VINCENT. Supt 35 Sprs. & four N.C.O's. under the Engr. Officer relieved work as on the defences of NEVEZON FARM.	
	1.12.1917		During the night 30.11.17 the Coy dug a fire trench 30 yds N.E. of CHOIX WITH COSE and strengthened existing wire.	
	2.12.1917		During night of 1.2.12.17 the Coy were employed on wiring Strong points	
	3.12.		The night 2/3.12.17 was spent digging a fire trench north of NEVEZON FARM and excepted the French defenses. work	
	4.12.		During night 3/4.12.17. The Coy. Were employed wiring the trenches round NEVEZON FARM. At 8 A.M. on the 4th the Coy. returned to HEUDICOURT and was not required again for either work or garrison duty.	

MAJOR, R.E.
COMMANDING 69th (FIELD) COMPANY R.E.

WAR DIARY
INTELLIGENCE SUMMARY.
(Erase heading not required.)

Army Form C. 2118.

Instructions regarding War Diaries and Intelligence Summaries are contained in F. S. Regs., Part II. and the Staff Manual respectively. Title pages will be prepared in manuscript.

Place	Date	Hour	Summary of Events and Information	Remarks and references to Appendices
CRETIGNY	5.12.1917.		Mounted Personnel assembled at CRETIGNY.	
BOUZINCOURT	6.		Coy. entrained at TINCOURT for BERGUETTE and marched to camp between Albert and Bouzincourt.	
	7.		Resting at "	
WITTERNESSE	8.		Coy. entrained at AUXEY for BERGUETTE and marched from Berguette to WITTERNESSE arriving with Billets about 8-7 P.M.	
	9.		Cleaning up and Kit inspections	
	10.		"	
GUARBECQUE	11.		Coy. marched from Witternesse to Guarbecque.	
	12.		Paraded to move off and received orders whilst on parade to postpone move.	
FOUQUEROU	13.		Coy. marched from Guarbecque to billets in FOUQUEROU.	
	14.		Drills & improvements to billets	
	15.		Gas Drill, Squad Drill, & Kit exercises & Physical Drill.	
	16.		"	
	17.		Pontoon & Trestle Drill on land.	
	18/19.			
	20.		Drawing new clothing, Drills, Tools, Haversacks & Satchels	
	21/22.		Witnessing on Rifles	
	23.		Sunday. Rest	
	24.		Building & reconstructing on Rates	
	25.		Christmas Day.	

J. Edwards
MAJOR, R.E.
COMMANDING 69th (FIELD) COMPANY R.E.

Army Form C. 2118.

WAR DIARY
or
INTELLIGENCE SUMMARY.

(Erase heading not required.)

Instructions regarding War Diaries and Intelligence Summaries are contained in F. S. Regs., Part II. and the Staff Manual respectively. Title pages will be prepared in manuscript.

Place	Date	Hour	Summary of Events and Information	Remarks and references to Appendices
MERVILLE	26.12.1917.		Coy. marched from HOULERON to MERVILLE.	
LES 3 TILLEULS	27.		Coy. marched from MERVILLE to LES 3 TILLEULS. nr ARMENTIERES.	
	28		Improving billets.	
	29 / 30 / 31		Working under C.E. XV Corps on defences. Wiring and concrete shelters.	

J. Ingram
MAJOR, R.E.
COMMANDING 69th (FIELD) COMPANY R.E.

12th DIVISIONAL ENGINEERS

69th FIELD COMPANY R. E.

JANUARY 1918

28031 W3125/M2250 1000m 6/17 M.R.Co.,Ltd. (1367) Forms W3091.   Army Form W. 3091.

Cover for Documents.

CONFIDENTIAL.

Nature of Enclosures.

WAR   DIARY

OF.

69TH. FIELD COY R.E.

Notes, or Letters written.

FROM 1.1.18   31.1.18

(VOLUME. 32)

Army Form C. 2118.

WAR DIARY
or
INTELLIGENCE SUMMARY.

(Erase heading not required.)

Instructions regarding War Diaries and Intelligence Summaries are contained in F. S. Regs., Part II. and the Staff Manual respectively. Title pages will be prepared in manuscript.

Place	Date	Hour	Summary of Events and Information	Remarks and references to Appendices
ESQ. 3 TILLEULS NR. ARMENTIERES.	1/1/18 to 15/1/18		Working under C.E. XV Corps on concrete emplacements and wiring reserve defences.	
FORT ROMPU	16/1/18		Coy moved to Billets near FORT ROMPU & took over work from 123rd Field Coy R.E.	
" "	7/1/18 to 31/1/18		One Section employed in the line supervising maintenance of trenches. Remainder, erecting footbaths & concrete shelters, repairing TIN BARN Avenue and roads in forward Area, repairing road screens, digging posts in reserve line of defence etc.	

E. Mann Capt. R.E.
Commanding 69th (FIELD) ARMY R.E.

12th DIVISIONAL ENGINEERS

69th FIELD COMPANY R. E.

FEBRUARY 1918

CONFIDENTIAL

28031 W3125/M2250 1000m 6/17 M.R.Co.,Ltd. (1367) Forms W3091. Army Form W. 3091.

Cover for Documents.

Nature of Enclosures.

WAR DIARY

OF

69ᵀᴴ FIELD Coy RE

Notes, or Letters written.

1·2·18   TO   28·2·18

(VOLUME 33)

Army Form C. 2118.

WAR DIARY
or
INTELLIGENCE SUMMARY

(Erase heading not required.)

Instructions regarding War Diaries and Intelligence Summaries are contained in F. S. Regs., Part II, and the Staff Manual respectively. Title pages will be prepared in manuscript.

Place	Date	Hour	Summary of Events and Information	Remarks and references to Appendices
Fort Rompu	1.2.1918	24.00	Working on left Brigade Area in F Div. on:- excavation of posts in 1st VESICA switch line, and FLEURBAIX - L'ARMEE LINE, breech shelters wiring FLEURBAIX - L'ARMEE LINE, excavating and clearing rifle line.	Sheet No.
H.B.E.G.	23.2.1918	do.	For. Orders, alterations to Brigade Baths, maintenance of trenches, maintenance of screens, filling in shell hole on forward roads, clearing roads, remaking of emergency roads, laying lines and wire entanglements to be demolition of Fort 31 Manor Farm and taking out practice trenches continued.	
	13.2.1918		Bridge mobilization carried out before rival work	
			1. O.R. wounded 23.2.18.	

J. Tugwell
MAJOR R.E.
COMMANDING 69th FIELD COMPANY R.E.

12th Divisional Engineers

WAR DIARY

69th FIELD COMPANY R. E.

MARCH 1 9 1 8

28031 W3125/M2250 1000m 6/17 M.R.Co.,Ltd. (1367) Forms W3091.   Army Form W.3091.

Cover for Documents.

Confidential

Nature of Enclosures.

War   Diary

of

69th Field Coy R.E.

From 1.3.18   31.3.18

Notes, or Letters written.

(Volume 34)

WAR DIARY or INTELLIGENCE SUMMARY

Army Form C. 2118.

Place	Date	Hour	Summary of Events and Information	Remarks and references to Appendices
FORT ROMPU H.13.B.3.6	18/3/18		Work on LEFT BRIGADE Area 2nd Down in Execution & onto positions by making & running ammunition recesses. LA VESEE SWITCH LINE and	
"	to		FLEURBAIX & ARMÉE LINE cement shelters. Wiring cemetery A.D.S. shelter and alteration to Bath WOR, making Emergency Artillery Road Truck maintenance, rehearse of company & drawing and filling in	
"			shell holes on roads.	
"	19/3/18		1 O.R. wounded on 11.3.18	
"	20/3/18		Sgt Lewis sent to 505 FIELD Coy RE	
"	"		Company moved to New Billets at ERQUINGHEM work taken over from 505 FIELD Coy RE under C.R.E. XV Corps Troops	
ERQUINGHEM	21/3/18		Evert War Office Instructions 1 O.R. Gassed. Employed Boulangerie	
H.8.B.10.3			Late in Camp	
"	22/3/18		Work on Enemy Machine Gun positions to commence. Working Parties received to stand by in readiness to move	
"	23/3/18		TRANSPORT moved by road to LE SART	
"	24/3/18		Remainder of Company marched to LEVERRIER & embussed there at 10 a.m. for	

Army Form C. 2118.

WAR DIARY
or
INTELLIGENCE SUMMARY.
(Erase heading not required.)

Instructions regarding War Diaries and Intelligence Summaries are contained in F. S. Regs., Part II. and the Staff Manual respectively. Title pages will be prepared in manuscript.

No 2

Place	Date	Hour	Summary of Events and Information	Remarks and references to Appendices
OBLINGHEM	24/3/18		OBLINGHEM (Cyclists paraded by order)	
"	"		TRANSPORT left from LE SART to OBLINGHEM	
OBLINGHEM	"		Remainder of Battalion of Coy. left OBLINGHEM about 8.30 pm and marched to FOUQUIERES and entrained en route for BOUZINCOURT detraining about	
"	"	11 am on 25/3/18		
"	25/3/18		TRANSPORT moved from OBLINGHEM to MINGOVAL	
BOUZINCOURT	"		Company starting to hold line Y E of BOUZINCOURT in case of enemy advance	
"	26/3/18		Digging bridge water cable & water pumping station in ALBERT & East of ALBERT & standing to N E of village	
"	"		TRANSPORT moved from MINGOVAL to LUCHEUX	
"	27/3/18		Coy. stood to N E of village & night transport moved from LUCHEUX to FRESSEVILLE	
"	28/3/18		Enemy who had got in BOUZINCOURT (Cavalry & Infantry) & IPS wounded & 3 ORS killed. Remainder hoped from BOUZINCOURT to HEDAUVILLE & digging Corps line at night	
HEDAUVILLE	29/3/18		Dismounted portion of Company hoped from HEDAUVILLE to WARLOY digging Corps line at night	

Army Form C. 2118.

WAR DIARY
or
INTELLIGENCE SUMMARY.
(Erase heading not required.)

Place	Date	Hour	Summary of Events and Information	Remarks and references to Appendices
WARLOY	30/3/18	A.M	Heavy & highly enemy fire along pt.	
"	"		TRANSPORT moved from FORCEVILLE to WARLOY	
"	31/3/18		Heavy & highly enemy shelling at night	

J. Twyner Major, R.E.
COMMANDING 69th (FIELD) COMPANY R.E.

12th Div.

69th FIELD COMPANY, R.E.

A P R I L

1 9 1 8

Army Form C. 2118.

WAR DIARY
or
INTELLIGENCE SUMMARY.
(Erase heading not required.)

Place	Date	Hour	Summary of Events and Information	Remarks and references to Appendices
57D 1/4 to 10/4				
WARLOY	1/4/18		Work at night. Wiring & digging Corps Line Y.18.A.B.+C.	
"	2/4/18		Dismounted portion of Coy moved to SENLIS. Work handed over to 78th Field Coy R.E. New work reconnoitred taken over from 78th Field Coy R.E.	
SENLIS	3/4/18		Coy paraded in morning for Inspections & Fatigues on Billets. Work at night, digging FRONT LINE & SUPPORT LINE Trench E.3 a 8 5 W. of ALBERT.	
"	4/4/18		Work by night on FRONT LINE. W.27.c.8.4. & E.3.a.5.6. W. of ALBERT. Warning orders received by 3.45 a.m. to stand to in Billets by 6 a.m. Enemy bombardment commenced 7 A.M. Dismounted portion of Coy moved forward to hold part of Corps. Line W. of BOUZINCOURT under O.C. 5th Northants Regt. Casualties: 1 O.R. Killed + 6 Wounded.	
"	5/4/18			
"	"			
"	"			
"	6/4/18		Dismounted still standing to till 12 Noon, when they returned to Billets at SENLIS. Orders received from Town Major SENLIS. 8 PM to evacuate billets, then moved to and Bivouaced in open at V.10.central. Casualties. 2 O.R's killed. 1 O.R. W'ded	
"	7/4/18 to 10/4/18		Coy wiring at night on FRONT LINE. & strengthening existing wire & fort Storage Points and excavations	
"	11/4/18		Work handed over to 161 Field Coy R.E. Coy moved to WARLOY at 1 PM, & took over work from 78th Field Coy R.E. Work reconnoitred & trenches taken out on ARMY SUPPORT Line V.7.A.	

Cont'd

Contd/

Army Form C. 2118.

WAR DIARY
~~INTELLIGENCE SUMMARY~~
(Erase heading not required.)

Instructions regarding War Diaries and Intelligence Summaries are contained in F. S. Regs., Part II, and the Staff Manual respectively. Title pages will be prepared in manuscript.

Place	Date	Hour	Summary of Events and Information	Remarks and references to Appendices
57 D 1/40000				
WARLOY	12/4/18		Coy employed digging ARMY Support Line Y.7.A. & Y.7.C.	
"	13/4/18		Coy parade - Kit Inspection. Baths	
"	14/4/18 & 15/4/18		Digging, Wiring & Draining ARMY Front Line Y.7.A. & Y.7.C.	
"	16/4/18		Coy Parade. Rifle & Gas helmet inspection. Fatigues & recreation	
"	17/4/18 & 18/4/18		Work on FRONT Line BAIZIEUX Defences in U.29 & U.30	
"	19/4/18		Rifle. Box Respirator Inspection from Rates & Ammunition Inspection	
"			Night work on HENENCOURT defences D.3. & D.4.	
"	20/4/18		Fatigues	
"	21/4/18 & 22/4/18		Digging FRONT Line BAIZIEUX Defences in U.29 & U.30 & Front Line D.3 & D.4, and ARMY SUPPORT Line Y.7.	
"	23/4/18		Coy parade for Baths. Recreation in afternoon	
"	24/4/18		" " " Fatigue. Moved to Billets in ACHEUX, & work taken over from 1st New Zealand Fld Coy R.E. in line — TRANSPORT Line at P.13. 13.7.7.	
ACHEUX	25/4/18 & 27/4/18		Digging Front Line trench (PURPLE Line) at P.10.d. Casualties on 26.4.18 OR Killed & 7 OR W'd'd.	
"	28/4/18 & 29/4/18		Coy work on (BLUE LINE) FRONT LINE. Digging trench from Q.8. D.2.5. to Q.14. 13.1.7. Casualties 1 OR Killed.	
"	30/4/18		" " to " to Q.14. D to Q.14. D & Q.14.	

M.R. Ramsden
Major
O.C. 69th (FIELD) COMPANY R.E.

12th DIVISONAL ENGINEERS

69th FIELD COMPANY R.E.

MAXY 1918

2803 W3125/M2250 1000m 6/17 M.R.Co.,Ltd. (1367) Forms W3091.   Army Form W. 3091.

CONFIDENTIAL
Cover for Documents.

Vol 33

Nature of Enclosures.

WAR   DIARY

OF

69th FIELD Coy RE

Notes, or Letters written.

FROM 1/5/18   31/5/18.

(VOLUME 36)

WAR DIARY
or
INTELLIGENCE SUMMARY

Army Form C. 2118.

Place	Date	Hour	Summary of Events and Information	Remarks and references to Appendices
Sheet 57D/&NW				
ACHEUX	May 1st	1918	Work on Dugout Front Line (Blue system) Q.14.d. One Section employed in line	
	2nd		supervising maintenance of trenches & wiring until further notice. (Billeted in MAILLY MAILLET Q.7.a.2.2)	
	3rd		Work on dugout Front Line (Purple system) Q.14.	
	4th		do. do. Wiring from Q.15.c.9.0 - Q.15 Central	
			Q.15.a.7.6. - Blowing graters for obstruction in Road Q.6.d.9.6.8. Transport moved to line Q.6.c.c - OP w'd out	
	5th		Work on dugout Front Line (Purple system) Q.8.d. & supporting points to Front Line Q.14.a.2.2.	
			Marking Emergency Posts "A" system notices boards & ramping banks.	
	6th & 7th		Making Finishing Front Line (Auchonvillers Line) Q.15.c Northwards & Dugging Front Line (Purple system) Q.14.a.	
			Dugging Front Line & supporting line Q.14.c. (Purple system)	
	8th		Filling in trenches in front of Auchonvillers switch Q.9.9.6.11. Q.8.8.D.3.4. Digging Front Line Q.14.c	
	9th		Work on Auchonvillers switch supporting points & wiring between points Q.8.a.	
	10th		Wiring switch Q.15.e.7.6 - Q.15.a.7.1 Q.15.a.4.4.	
	11th		Work on Auchonvillers switch & Front Line & Splitlocking C.T. Q.14.a.	
			Digging missing portion Auchonvillers switch & CT for Purple system Q.8.d. Wiring intervals between	
			supporting points Q.14.c. & Dugging Front Line Q.8.2.8.1 - CT Q.14.a. Excavating for New Billets P.11.c.5.8.	
	12th		Wiring Posts Q.14.c. & Dugging Front Line Q.8.2.8.1 - CT Q.14.a. (Purple system) Work on New Billets	
	13th		Dugging CT Q.14.a. fixing posts on Emergency Track "A"	
			Coy moved to Billets P.11.c.5.9. Work on Q.8.d + CT Q.14.a. (Purple system)	
BEAUSSART	14th		Reconnaissance & marking out tracks alongside of Louvencourt - Acheux & Leavillers Roads & until further notice	
	15th & 16th		Dugging & drawing Front Line Q.8.d. + CT Q.14.a. (Purple system)	
	17th		" deepening sumps & making steps Work on CT from Front Line to supporting posts Q.14.a.	
			& switch line Q.14.c.	
	18th & 19th		Dugging CT Q.14.a. Drawing Front Line Wiring CT Q.14.c. + R.14.c (Purple system)	
	20th		" " Q.14.d. Salving Wire (Brown line) " " Sector employed in line beyond Coy	
	21st		Coy standing to in reserve (Brown Line)	
	22nd & 23rd		Dugging CT in Q.14.D. (Purple system) Dugging CT- Q.14.a.	
	24th		Drawing Front Line (Purple system) By day 78th Field Coy R.E. Tracks in Louvencourt Acheux Leavillers roads & complete.	
	25th		Handed our work to 78th Field Coy R.E.	
PUCHEVILLERS	26th		Coy & Transport moved to PUCHEVILLERS	
	27th to 31st		Training Physical Musketry Signal drill & Field Works. (Overland & Lectures)	

Major R.E.
O.C. 94th Field Company R.E.

12th DIVISIONAL ENGINEERS

69th FIELD COMPANY R. E.

JUNE 1918

Vol 34

2803... W3125/M2250 1000m 6/17 M.R.Co.,Ltd. (1367) Forms W3091   Army Form W.3091.

Cover for Documents.

CONFIDENTIAL

Nature of Enclosures.

WAR   DIARY

69TH FIELD COY R.E.

Notes, or Letters written.

From 1·6·18   To 29·6·18

(VOLUME 37)

Army Form C. 2118.

WAR DIARY
or
INTELLIGENCE SUMMARY
(Erase heading not required.)

Place	Date	Hour	Summary of Events and Information	Remarks and references to Appendices
SHEET 27 D/Appx 1				
PUCHEVILLERS	1/6/18		TRAINING. Musketry on Range at ARQUEVES.	
ACHEUX	2/6/18		Coy moved to Camp at O.12.d.1.5. Reconnaissance of work taken over from 81st Field Coy RE and CE./Corps.	
	3/6/18 & 4.6.18		Work on Acheux Front Line & Switch. O.4 act ʎ Reserve Line Q.7 ʎ (PURPLE SYSTEM) Instructy Cy. ʎ 3 Offrs.	
PUCHEVILLERS	5/6/18		Orders received to move to PUCHEVILLERS	
	6/6/18 & 15/6/18		Coy Training for Open Warfare — Extended Order Drill Musketry. Demolition etc. Coy moved completed at 9 am. Coy standing to under orders to move	
	16/6/18		Work taken over from 204 Field Coy RE & reconnoitred	
	17/6/18		Coy went to New Battle at Y.2.d.4.b. Transport Lines at U.11.c.2.7.	
CAMP V.3.d.4.6	18/6/18		Coy employed in Line — BOUZINCOURT TR — (PURPLE SYSTEM) Cleaning out trench & improving berms. Extension W.1.d.3.4.1. Work D.O.P. adjacent Chalk Pit Q.31.c.7.7 continuing Bouzincourt Ave. W.14.a.7.7	
	19/6/18		Bouzincourt Support — V.12.d.65.15. Deepening Trench Northwards & cleaning up TR at W.1.d.3.4	
	20.6.18		Widening TR W.13.b.2.2 Southwards. Wiring from W.13.b.5.3 to W.13.b.1.1	
	21/6/18 & 22/6/18		As on 20 of — .... Also wiring BOUZINCOURT AVE. W.13.a.4.7.3	
	22.6/18		Wiring TR W.13.b.1.0 to W.13.c.10.9 & W.7.b.5.9 Southwards.	
	23.6.18		Digging TR W.13.d.12.2.5 W.13.b.6.4.3 — Widening & deepening Support TR Y.13 & Y.12	
	24.6.18 & 25.6.18		Extension of Trench in W.13.a.4.7	
			Dig Cup BOUZINCOURT TR W.13.b.to — Deepening BOUZINCOURT AVE — Laying TR BOARDS. Extension of Tracks in W.13.	
	26.6.18		BOUZINCOURT TR. W.13.a & b. Screening.... Deepening TR W.13.b.5.4 & Support TR Y.18 Q.31.d .... Widening & deepening .... BOUZINCOURT AVE. Deepening. Laying TR Boards	
	27.6.18 & 28.6.18		& Revmt. Work on Batling Bay on ALBERT·BOUZINCOURT ROAD. fixing heavy plate & widening	
	29.6.18		Bouzincourt A.R.E. ... Laying Trench Boards. One Section practising for operation.	

W. Alexander
Major
69th (Field) Company R.E.

12th DIVISIONAL ENGINEERS

69th FIELD COMPANY R. E.

JULY 1916

Vol 35

(6339) Wt. W160/M3016 1,500,000 10/17 McA & W Ltd (E1898) Forms W3091.   Army Form W.3091.

CONFIDENTIAL

Cover for Documents.

Nature of Enclosures.

WAR   DIARY

OF

69th FIELD Coy RE

Notes, or Letters written.

From 30.6.18   To 30.7.18

(VOLUME 38)

WAR DIARY or INTELLIGENCE SUMMARY

Army Form C. 2118.

Place	Date	Hour	Summary of Events and Information	Remarks and references to Appendices
57 d/NE/10 Y.2.b.			One Section in Co-operation with Infantry in attack on Bouzincourt Ridge L.W.15.a + B. P.W.15.a + B. P.W.15 d 2.6 - 4 O.R. Rank employed in demolition in enemy Dug-outs etc. - Casualties 10 O.R's wounded.	
New Hedauville	30.6.18		One Section employed on construction of Adv But H.Q'rs V.7.a - Excavations erecting shelters for HQ offrs. Cemp.Hqrs etc and also on Battery at V.16 a 8.8 - Framing shelters wiring supporting revetting expanding + etc to improve	
	1.7.18		Remainder of Coy - BOUZINCOURT AVE. supply Camel Beach wiring, reclaim under road etc to improve field of fire.	
			One Section employed on Adv Dug-out + B. W. Sanston. to L.15 - Remainder of Coy standing by as lines for further	
			wiring. Work made impossible owing to enemy fire.	
	2.7.18		One Section employed on Adv Dug-outs + Baths as on 1st inst. - Wiring party standing by on line - Work impossible owing to enemy counter attack. - Remainder of Coy. BOUZINCOURT AVE. erecting (?)+ etc as on 1st inst.	
	3.7.18		One Section in Adv to HQ's Where as usual. Remainder Coy employed BOUZINCOURT AVE as on 2nd. Existing trench + Royal W.1.d. - Adv wiring Butter P 33 d. 7. 9. Excavation of Bath.	
	4.7.18		As on 2nd inst.	
	5.7.18		Part Coy employed digging C.T. between BOUZINCOURT SUPPORT W.16.2.1. + BOUZINCOURT TR. W.1 d 5.9 - tunnelling BOUZINCOURT AVE + BOUZINCOURT TR. 17 remainder employed constructing Adv R.A.P. 48ª baths. Adv Dressing Station at Y.15.a.3.8. + P 33 a.7.9.	
	6.7.18		Part Coy employed + fatigue Ct. between BOUZINCOURT SUPPORT W.15.b.1 + W.1 d 6.19. BOUZINCOURT AVE. erecting wire entanglement + improving field of fire as before. Remainder in Adv Bat'n dug-out Baths at W.1.B.33ª as usual.	
	7.7.18		As on 6th inst. + Excavation of M.G. Emplacements Y.13 a. 6.2. Part Coy employed on tunnelling BOUZINCOURT TR W.1 b.7.2. + improving BOUZINCOURT SUPPORT + remainder constructing Adv Dut HQ's Baths + A.D.S. as before. - 1 O.R. wounded on D.A.	
	8.7.18 + 9.7.18		Work handed over to 204 Field Coy R.E. Coy moved to RUBEMPRE.	
Rubempre	10.7.18		Refitting + reorganising + improving camp etc.	
	11.7.12 + 7.18			
	13/7/18		Warning Orders received to be prepared to move. - Transport less Toolcarts proceeded to RENANCOURT. Remainder of Coy + Transport standing by for further instructions.	
NAMPS AU MONT	14/7/18		TRANSPORT Buses from RENANCOURT to NAMP AU MONT. Remainder of Coy entrained for NAMPS AU MONT Toolcarts forwarded by train	
RUMIGNY	15/7/18		Coy march to billets at RUMIGNY	

Army Form C. 2118.

WAR DIARY
or
INTELLIGENCE SUMMARY.
(Erase heading not required.)

Place	Date	Hour	Summary of Events and Information	Remarks and references to Appendices
AMPLIER	17		Coy club parade. cleaning billets & other Coy fatigues	
RUMIGNY	16.7.18		Training	
	27.7.18	6.30pm	Warning Order received. Prepare to move	
LENS.I.	29.7.18			
HAYERNAS	30.7.18		Coy moved to HAYERNAS. Dismounted by Train. Mounted by Road.	

B.F. Leverington
MAJOR R.E.
COMMANDING 98th (F.) Coy. INFANTRY R.E.

12th Divisional Engineers

69th FIELD COMPANY,

ROYAL ENGINEERS,

AUGUST, 1918.

WAR DIARY
INTELLIGENCE SUMMARY

Army Form C. 2118.

Place	Date	Hour	Summary of Events and Information	Remarks and references to Appendices
HAVERNAS (Ref. Lens II) G.2.D.7 & D.13 D.19.a.3.2 Nr BRAIZIEUX	31.7.18/1/8/18		Coy Training. Reconnaissance & Refitting.	
	2.8.18		WARNING ORDER Received to be prepared to move – Coy Standing by for movement.	
	3.8.18		Dismounted portion moved by Bus to New Billets. D.19. a.1.2. (BRAIZIEUX) Transport by Road to BRAIZIEUX – Reconnoitring work taken over from 503 Field Coy R.E.	
	4.5.18		NIGHT WORK. Wiring Scheme Incorporating tunnel sh.1. Existing Posts from D.17.b.4.3 to D.17.b.4.3. Nr BRAIZIEUX	
			– D.17.c.3.8 & D.17.c.5.6. – WIDENING TR. DARWIN RES) D.17.b.1.7. Southwards ... DAY WORK – Testing Minto W.20.b. and W.21.a. – DARWIN COPSE – (DARWIN RES)	
	5.8.18		NIGHT WORK – WIDENING TR. DARWIN COPSE. D.17. DAILY WIRE Southerly Dugouts DARWIN COPSE	
	6.8.18	7.18	– D.17. DARLIS of a RECENT GARDENS Pot. Bretonon. H. New Bat Hq. & DARWIN RES. widening trench TR.	
			Anti-gas training Sep – 32057 7880 made R4 G.20 6.8.7. Salvg balloon & ferrying 2Lt.G. Walker ArtifeM.T.405	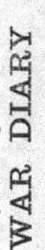
	7.8.18		By Days Trench & construction New Bridges D.19.a. 3.2	
	8.8.18		By Nights Barbed wire in Camp – Reconnoitering – (in Coys). Standing by for use of my Co. for purpose of	
	9.8.18		contributing stay posts in pending operation. 1 Officer seriously wounded.	
			Makeing ACTRY. POST. K.10.b.6.8 – Dismounted portion of Coy moved to BURNARM J9.6.7.5. 17 Dec 1917.	
J.9.6.7.5	10.8.18			
N.M. MERICOURT	11.8.18		Digging TRENCH & WIRING. CROSS POINT. K.10. b.3.3.	
	12.8.18/14.8.18		Clearing for Bde. H.Q. & constructing ramps. K.9.b.4.6.	
	15.8.18		On the 14th & marking TRACKS from K.3.c & K.4.a.2.4. – K.10.b.1.5. & K.5.c.9.8. and marking out trade from K.9.b.3.7.b.6. 6.8.5	
	16.9.18		constructing New Bdg. Nr 46a H.3.6.4.6.	
	17.8.18		" "	
	18.9.18		" "	Supporting Carrs – 2 Sections employed with Sch in Line – working filling & supporting it.
	19.8.18		On a 17" int – Wiring Ballet	
			Constructing Bde. H.O. N Infantry and other Bde. N.46a K.1.d.2.6. – Tigeary Road K.2.c.9.3. – making M.G. Shelter K.4.c.8.5.	
	20./21.8.18		Preparing Bridges K.1.d.3.6. Constructing plates Nr M.5 K.4.c.8.5. – Artry Bde. Hqrs K.9.d.4.6	
	22.9.18		Damaged railway lines at K.1.d.2.6. – 2 Sections employed on Tanks E.29.d. E.F.19.d. – 2 Sections to help in operations constructing line F.13.a. 2.2 to E.13.d.5.8 – Enemy Captured Bigade	
			Batty Traps – S. O.P.s wounded.	Cont.

WAR DIARY or INTELLIGENCE SUMMARY

Army Form C. 2118.

Place	Date	Hour	Summary of Events and Information	Remarks and references to Appendices
K.19.d.2.6 (AITZ)	23.8.18		Section never attached to Bn & for position and until further orders	
New Maricourt	24.8.18		BROWN LINE - Survey of Posts at F.2.5. - G.24.d - G.24.d - 10.4. & survey reports.	
	25.8.18		Cy moved to BUISSON E.12.B.9.6. - Employed work on wells. BECORDEL - and in burying own cable.	
E.12.d.8.5	26.8.18		Repairing Tracks & filling shell holes etc where necessary	
	27.8.18		As on 25th inst. + burying main cable to wells.	
BECORDEL	27.8.18		Construction of Track F.15.d. F.15.6. F.19.d. + F.19.d.2.2 making water troughs for power	
BECOURT			Filling in Shell holes, fixing water troughs - MAMETZ. Fitting up 8th Wilts Light HIDDEN WOOD. Collecting material + taking to dump at F.8.d.2.2. Digging horses + mules rampdowny m. site of dumps. Repairs to Wells, erecting troughs, pumps + making of filter troughlines. Cleaning approaches. Generally Impn. Construction of Track F.19 3.2 & CORPSE WOOD. Company repairing Tunnels suspected of being unsafe. - No damage found - Work on 8th Bn. BECORDEL on a 27th inst. getting material to Dump F.8.d.2.2. + making approaches to Same = erecting Bart home	
	28.8.18 to 29.8.18		BECORDEL. Work on Wells as before - maintenance lorry lorries Lorks + refilling pumps etc. Repairing Wells in HARDICOURT Area. + MAURIPAS System - running away etrays changed number,	
	30.8.13		+ tanks + overhauling pumps - renewing windlasses + company wells fit for use	

EWRamsden
Major R.E.

12th DIVISIONAL ENGINNERS

69th FIELD COMPANY R.E.

SEPTEMBER 1918

Army Form W.3091.

Vol 37

Cover for Documents.

CONFIDENTIAL

Nature of Enclosures.

WAR DIARY

OF

69th FIELD COY RE

Notes, or Letters written.

(VOLUME 40)

WAR DIARY or INTELLIGENCE SUMMARY.

Army Form C. 2118.

(Erase heading not required.)

Instructions regarding War Diaries and Intelligence Summaries are contained in F. S. Regs., Part II. and the Staff Manual respectively. Title pages will be prepared in manuscript.

Place	Date	Hour	Summary of Events and Information	Remarks and references to Appendices
E.12.d.8.5 BERCORDEL-BERCOURT	31.8.18 to 2/9/18		Coy employed on maintenance of wells, developing water supply, i.e. erecting windwheels, fixing pumps, troughs erecting Storage tank.	
	3/9/18		with apparatus received. MARICOURT Re-erecting CANVAS TANKS A.4.d.3.0. A.16.b.2.5. Salving tools & materials from outer defences AMIENS - 1 Section joined 35th Infan. Brigade for operations -	
FRECICOURT T.29.b.9.7	4/9/1918 5.9.1918		Coy and Transport moved to FRECICOURT - Engaged in operation on 5th. Bridging E. Tortille at MARAMCOURT where it crosses CANAL DU NORD. Existing BRIDGE repaired - VERY HEAVY ENEMY SHELLING. 3 O.R.s WOUNDED	
HENNUI'S WOOD	6/9/1918		Starting Bridges for H.T. at MARAMCOURT MILL - Removing & fixing CANVAS troughing and TANKS - Coy moved 3 Sections with Co. to HENNUI'S Wood	
T.2.C.8.2 W of NUREU.	7/9/1918		* Coy moved to BIVOUACS T.2.C.R.2 West of NUREU - TRANSPORT to T.11.a.1.2 near CANAL DU NORD - FLYING HORSE TROOPS 1 Section 2,800 gall. Tank near NUREU.	with Bde.
"	8/9/18		* Coy started new BRIDGE at MARAMCOURT MILL over CANAL DU NORD - SPAN 66 ft. - CRIB PIERS - ABUTMENTS - R.S.J.s as bearers. 1 Co. PIONEERS 5th. NORTHANTS employed on approaches.	
"	9/9/1918		Work on BRIDGE continued (Ready for TRANSPORT H.T. (5 Tons axle load) at 12. noon. (2) Small Bridges, 16 ft span. over TORTILLE R. completed - 5th. NORTHANTS (PIONEERS) working on approaches. 1 Section attached 35th. Bde. repaired MARAMCOURT MILL BRIDGE to NUREU filling shell holes & fixing MILES Beams -	
"	10/9/1918		Coy employed - improving track MARAMCOURT MILL BRIDGE to NUREU. Filling shell holes & fixing MILES Beams - Improving Billets	
"	11/9/1918		½ Co. employed on CORDUROY ROAD - as diversion to road MARAMCOURT BRIDGE - filling & levying ditches - 1 Section setting out practice trenches - 1 Section improving track Main Mill Bridge - remainder Billets	
"	12/9/1918		As on 11th. - Two Sections employed setting out practice Trenches for operations pending -	
"	13/9/18		½ Co. employed erecting New HQ for 35th. Bde at E.3.d. erecting Shelter, deepening approach trench. 60 shelter employed - ½ Co. employed on New Tramline H.G. T.16.C.1.9 (work done in conjunction with 70th. Field O.R.s)	
"	14/9/1918		As on 13.9.1918.	
"	15/9/1918		Graphoting to new Brigade H.Q. Completion - Coy Parades & Inspections - Baths -	
Dismounted Mounted E.14.C.5. 3¼ West of LIERAMONT	17/9/1918		Excavating & exploding charge for destroying enemy aerodrome bomb at NUREU T.4.b.2.8. Dismounted moved to Billets E.4.C.5.3. D.15. & L. Mounted to D.S.d.5.5. West of LIERAMONT - improving billets -	

WAR DIARY
or
INTELLIGENCE SUMMARY

Army Form C. 2118.

Place	Date	Hour	Summary of Events and Information	Remarks and references to Appendices
E.14.c.5.5. W. of FREMICOURT	18.9.18		1 Section attd. B & C Coy 12th M.G.C. in operation making Track – 1 OR killed 2 OR wounded – Making Horse Transport Track E.3.d.0.5. N.30.b.2.3. & from F.7.c.11.7. to F.7.a.8.0. Improving Roads N.30.b.2.6. & F.1. Central – Filling Shell holes & making pits for Horse Transport.	
	19.9.18		Making two Strong points in CHESTNUT AVENUE – 26. C.3.6. Repairing & draining SAULCOURT – PEIZIERES Road and thro' PEIZIERES & EPEHY	
	20/21.9.18		Repairing SAULCOURT – PEIZIERES Road – 2 Section standing by for work on Strong points. Finishing operation. Excavations E.4.c.1.8.8. New Bde H.Q. E.12.c.2.1. Bivouacs & pattern	
	22.9.18		1/2 Coy moved to Buirsmon	
E.14.c.2.8.8	23.9.18		1/2 Coy employed repairing & draining SAULCOURT-PEIZIERES Road E.14.c.0.6. & F.6.10.7.6. – remainder Coy on New Bde H.Q. E.12.c.2.1. – 3 Shelter. Conference erected – Salvage & collecting material	
W. of EPEHY	24.9.18		Coy employed Bde. H.Qrs. E.12.b.2.1. & Front Battn H.Qrs. F.9.a.1.8. & Erecting Shelter Repairs to SAULCOURT – PEIZIERES Road	
	25/26.9.18		On 24th Making New Bde H.Qrs. E.1.0.8.0. & Front Battn H.Qrs. F.3.c.1.0. – draining SAULCOURT PEIZIERES Road & repair to Road F.1. Central & F.15. & F.7.8. & bys Road F.15. b.1.0.	
	27.9.18		to F.15.b.7.6. & F.15.b.6.5. Making pits for Horse transport	
	28.9.18		Repairs to Roads E.10.C.10.8. & E.6.10.d.7.6.3. Making Tracks from MAY COPSE to EMPIRE POST E.9.a.6.1. to F.10.a.5.5. & Tracks for M.T. F.10.d.5.1. Road to EMPIRE POST E.9.a.6.1 to F.10.a.5.5. & Tracks for M.T. F.10.d.5.1. Road to EMPIRE POST filling shell holes, building thro' secondry tracks with Bricks (S.R.W.) etc.	
	29.9.18		Infantry Horse Transport Track F.9.a.6.1. to F.10.d.8.2. Running Pump. Installation EPEHY. 10.O.R. attached 35th Infan. Brigade for Operations	
	30.9.18		Standing by in reserve for operations 10.O.R.s rejoined from 35th Infan Brigade.	

30th. SEPT. 1918.

P.M. Cooper Capt. R.E.
a/OC. 65th Field C.R.E.

12th DIVISIONAL ENGINEERS

69th FIELD COMPANY R.E.

OCTOBER 1918

WO 38.

CONFIDENTIAL

WAR DIARY
OF 69th FIELD COY R.E.
OCTr 1st TO OCT 31st 1918

Army Form C. 2118.

Instructions regarding War Diaries and Intelligence Summaries are contained in F. S. Regs., Part II. and the Staff Manual respectively. Title pages will be prepared in manuscript.

WAR DIARY
or
INTELLIGENCE SUMMARY.
(Erase heading not required.)

Place	Date	Hour	Summary of Events and Information	Remarks and references to Appendices
	Oct. 1918			
	1st		Coy moved from Camp near EPEHY to CHUIGNOLLES via PERONNE. Dismounted bn. mounted by route march. Coy entrained 8 p.m.	
	2nd			
	3rd		Coy arrived AUBIGNY at 10 a.m. March to CAMBRAIN L'ABBEY	
	4 & 5		Unloading Kit & stores equipment at CAMBRAIN L'ABBEY	
	6th		Section moved to forward billet near THEUS, taking on work from 84 Fd Coy R.E. Transport returned to be TARGETTE.	
	7 & 8		3 Sections working on road repairs by night. One Section framing	
	9th		enemy returns. 2 Sub. at work on roads, 1 attached to 3/Bde HQ. 1 building new Div E. HQ. at AVION.	
	10th		Coy HQ and two Section moved to camp at PRIEUX. Work on roads reconnaissance of roads routes to forward area.	
	11th		No 1 section moved to billet in OROCOURT. Two section working on roads.	
	12th		Coy HQ and 3 sections moved to billet just East of HENIN LIETARD, and Transport lines to BILLY MONTIGNY. Coy starting by to put Pontoon Bridge across CANAL	
	13th		OG LA HAUTE DEULE	
	14th		3 Sections working on roads. 1 Sect with 35 Bde preparing portable footbridge to cross to CANAL OG LA HAUTE DEULE	

WAR DIARY
or
INTELLIGENCE SUMMARY
(Erase heading not required.)

Army Form C. 2118.

Instructions regarding War Diaries and Intelligence Summaries are contained in F. S. Regs., Part II. and the Staff Manual respectively. Title pages will be prepared in manuscript.

Place	Date	Hour	Summary of Events and Information	Remarks and references to Appendices
	15th & 16th		Work on roads & return arm arm & roads trestles to pontoon bridge.	
	17th		2 sections put pontoon bridge nr Canal at AUBY.	
	18th & 19th		Built Trestle bridge for H.T. across CANAL & pushed up pontoons. Coy HQ and Transport moved to Billets nr AUBY.	
	20th		Coy in reserve. 1 sect with 35 Bde: 1 working on roads: 1 on bridge maintenance and 1 sect in rest.	
	21st		Coy HQ, Sects & Transport moved to ORCHIES. 1 Sect. rejoined from 35 Bde.	
	22nd		Work on roads nr ORCHIES. Repairing craters.	
	23rd		Coy HQ, Sects & Transport moved to BOUR BOTIN. Sects working on roads.	
	24th & 25th and 26th		1 Sect attached to 37 Bde. 3 Sects & Transport standing by to put pontoon bridge over RIVER L'ESCAUT and JARD Canal. Work on roads near Billets.	
	27th		Sent with 37 Bde put foot bridge across RIVER L'ESCAUT.	
	28th		Coy relieved by 412 Field Coy R.E. & returned to BOUR BOTIN.	
	29th 30th 31st		Overhauling & cleaning equipment.	

Gulledge
Maj R.E.
On Oy 2nd Coy R.E.

12th DIVISIONAL ENGINEERS

69th FIELD COMPANY R.E.

NOVEMBER 1918

Vol 39

Army Form W.3091.

Cover for Documents.

CONFIDENTIAL

Nature of Enclosures.

WAR DIARY

OF

69th FIELD COY RE

FROM 1 11 18   30 11 18

Notes, or Letters written.

(VOLUME 42)

Army Form C. 2118.

WAR DIARY
or
INTELLIGENCE SUMMARY.
(Erase heading not required.)

Instructions regarding War Diaries and Intelligence Summaries are contained in F. S. Regs., Part II. and the Staff Manual respectively. Title pages will be prepared in manuscript.

69th FIELD COMPANY ROYAL ENGINEERS

Place	Date	Hour	Summary of Events and Information	Remarks and references to Appendices
	November 1918.			
	1st to 7th		Whole Company at BOUR BOTIN. Training.	
	8th to 9th		Coy. moves complete to ODOMEZ. Work on roads.	
	10th		Two section moves to BLATON to erect bridge over ANTOING Canal.	
	11th		Balance of Coy. moves to BLATON. Work on roads & bridges.	
	12th to 24th		Work on roads & bridges.	
	25th		Company moves to St. AMAND by march route.	
	26th		Company moves to ANICHE by march route.	
	27th to 30th		Work on billets and Divisional Workshops.	

Grinnell
Major R.E.
O.C. 69 Field Coy R.E.

12th DIVISIONAL ENGINEERS

69th FIELD COMPANY R.E.

DECEMBER 1918

28031 W3125/M2250 1000m 6/17 M.R.Co.,Ltd. (1367) Forms W3091.   Army Form W. 3091.

CONFIDENTIAL
Cover for Documents.

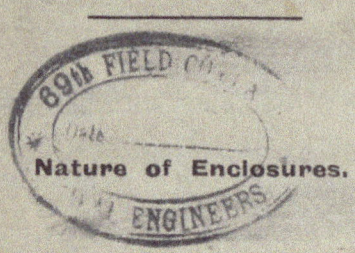

Nature of Enclosures.

WAR DIARY

OF

69TH FIELD COY RE

From 1/12/18   To 31/12/18

Notes, or Letters written.

(VOLUME 42)

Army Form C. 2118.

WAR DIARY
or
INTELLIGENCE SUMMARY.

(Erase heading not required.)

Instructions regarding War Diaries and Intelligence Summaries are contained in F. S. Regs., Part II. and the Staff Manual respectively. Title pages will be prepared in manuscript.

Place	Date	Hour	Summary of Events and Information	Remarks and references to Appendices
ANICHE	December 1918			
	1st to 6th		Work on billets & Divisional Workshops.	
	7th to 8th		32 NCOs & men commenced work on Demobilization Camp at SOMAIN. Remainder - Work on billets & Divisional Workshops.	
	9th		Educational Classes started for (a) Building Construction (b) Mechanical Eng g (c) Elementary Education (a) French. Work continues on Camp at SOMAIN for billets	
	10th to 13th		As for 9th Dec.	
	14th to 15th		Musketry Training under arrangements of O.C. Coy (except party working on camp at SOMAIN) As for 9th to 13th Dec.	
	16th to 18th		Party on Camp at SOMAIN reduced to 1 S & Work commenced on New Bath House at SOMAIN & Solder Kiln at BE a.4.8. Other work as for 9th - 13th Dec.	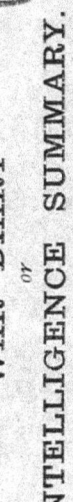
	19th to 20th		Coy parades for Inspection &c.	
	21st		Regimental parade under C.R.E.	
	23rd		Inspection of Divl. R.E. by G.O.C. 12th Divn.	
	24th to 25th		Holiday	
	26th		Work on Bath House at SOMAIN, Refilling point for A.S.C. in SOMAIN SQUARE.	
	27th to 31st			

Vol 41

CONFIDENTIAL

Cover for Documents.

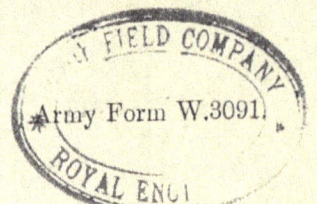

WAR DIARY

Nature of Enclosures.

OF

69" FIELD Coy RE

From 1.1.19   To 31.1.19

Notes, or Letters written.

(VOLUME 44)

WAR DIARY
INTELLIGENCE SUMMARY

Army Form C. 2118.

Place	Date	Hour	Summary of Events and Information	Remarks and references to Appendices
ANICHE	1st to 31st Jan. 1919		Company working on Bath House and Disinfector at SOMAIN and wiring room at SOMAIN STATION for Demobilization Camp. No of Men demobilized to date 54 O.R. 1 Officer	

G. H. Hold Major R.E.

MAJOR, R.E.,
COMMANDING 69th (FIELD) COY. R.E.

Army Form W.3091.

Cover for Documents.

CONFIDENTIAL

Nature of Enclosures.

WAR DIARY

OF

69th FIELD Coy RE

From 1.2.19 To 28.6.19

Notes, or Letters written.

(Volume 4.4)

WAR DIARY
or
INTELLIGENCE SUMMARY.

Army Form C. 2118.

Place	Date	Hour	Summary of Events and Information	Remarks and references to Appendices
	1919.			
ANICHE	1st Feby to 28th Feby		Coy. working on Both Areas at SOMAIN also building and raising tracks at ANICHE. Major G H KOHL reports to Divisional Canadian Coy for demobilisation (repatriating) — taken over by Capt L.A. HALSALL Numbers dwindling to date — officers 3 O.R. 86 Also 18 horses dispatched to ease + repatriation	

M Halsall Capt
O.C. 69th Field Coy C.E.

Cover for Documents.

Vol 33

CONFIDENTIAL

Nature of Enclosures,

WAR DIARY

OF

69th FIELD COY R.E

From 1 3 19   To 31 3 19

Notes, or Letters written,

(VOLUME 46)

WAR DIARY or INTELLIGENCE SUMMARY

Army Form C. 2118.

Place	Date	Hour	Summary of Events and Information	Remarks and references to Appendices
ANICHE	March 1st to 31st 1919		Coy. working on Both Horse ated Draughter at "SOMAIN" shed, were completed on 22nd Mar. Also on entrained ramps & transport. Ramps at ANICHE STAIN - completed 26th Mar. Rest demobilised to date - officers 3 O.R. 20 Lt Butler proceeded to No 3 defence works centre WEST RIDING for duty 29/3/19 Lt English posted to No 5 B.R. centre KAMBS proceded 4th 24th 3/19. The Company was down to Cadre "A" strength on 27.3.19.	

Maria Capt
OC 69th Field Coy RE

(6392) Wt. W6192/PS75 1,500,000 4/18 McA & W Ltd (E 2815) Forms W3091/4.   Army Form W.3091.

Cover for Documents.

CONFIDENTIAL

Nature of Enclosures.

WAR DIARY

OF

69ᵗʰ FIELD COY R.E.

FROM 1.4.19   TO 30.4.19

Notes, or Letters written.

(VOLUME 47)

Army Form C. 2118.

WAR DIARY
INTELLIGENCE SUMMARY
(Erase heading not required.)

Instructions regarding War Diaries and Intelligence Summaries are contained in F. S. Regs., Part II. and the Staff Manual respectively. Title pages will be prepared in manuscript.

Place	Date	Hour	Summary of Events and Information	Remarks and references to Appendices
ANICHE	1st to 30 April 1919		Coy. stationed at Aniche awaiting orders to proceed to England as cadre. No work in progress with exception of interior economy work of Coy. Such as checking stores &c. Strength on 30/4/19 — 2 Officers, 53 O.R's. Total 55	
	16/4/19		11 O.R's despatched to CRE. 6th Divn for service with A. of O.	
	22/4/19		Lt. H.G. THOMAS M.C. proceeded for duty with No. 5 Defence Sector NAMUR.	

M. Maclean Capt
O.C. 69th Field Coy R.E.

(A9175) Wt W2358/P360 600,000 12/17 D. D. & L. Sch 88a. Forms/C2118/15

Army Form W.3091.

Cover for Documents.

CONFIDENTIAL.

Nature of Enclosures.

WAR DIARY

OF

69th FIELD COY RE

FROM 1/5/19   TO 31/5/19

Notes, or Letters written.

(Volume 48.)

Army Form C. 2118.

WAR DIARY
or
INTELLIGENCE SUMMARY.
(Erase heading not required.)

Place	Date	Hour	Summary of Events and Information	Remarks and references to Appendices
ANICHE FRANCE.	1st to 31st MAY 1919		Cadre of Company awaiting orders to proceed to England. No work in progress, with exception of guard duties over Coy stores vehicles etc. 10.5.19 10 O.R's sent to Concentration Camp for demobilization reducing cadre to 2 Officers 40 O.R's (as per D.A.G. HQ. CR.3172/(Mob) — 29.4.19) Total demobilised to date. 3 Officers & 96 O.R's	

M Cassall Capt
O.C. 69th Field Co R.E.

69th FIELD COMPANY — ROYAL ENGINEERS — Date 31/5/19

18.40/2

70th Field Coy R.E.

12TH DIVISION

70TH FIELD COY R.E.

MAY 1915 - MAY 1919

70² F.C.D.E.
Vol. I

D/
7678

13th Durham

From May to Oct. 15.

may 15

Confidential.

War-Diary

of

70th Field Company R.E.

from May 31st 1915 to Oct 31st 1915.

(Volume 1)

Chap. 1.   13

(70th FD Co.R.E.)

May 31st Monday. Entrain Farnborough. L.S.W.Ry.
    & Co. 7.20.am. & 8.20am.
    Arrive " 9.0. am. 10. am. Southampton

June 1st in Havre. Early morning.
    Concentrate, make up Deficiencies from Ordnance
    & Remounts, & draw rations.
    Entrain 10.30 pm.

June 2nd W.D. — DUCHY. 8.am.
    Company Strength 6. Offrs.
                        223 men
                        87 Horses
                        16 vehicles.

June 3rd Detrain St. OMER. 9.45pm 10.45 pm. march off
    10.45 pm. Reach SETQUES 12.45 pm.
    Billeted in 2 farm barns.
    HdQrs Inf. Bde 35th QUELMES.
    Cleaning up, Drill exercises.

June 4th Exercises, Drill & swimming parades.
    Cleaning carts & harness.
    Acquiring billets routine.
    Orders to be prepared to march tomorrow.

June 5th Saturday. March from SETQUES to
    LA BELLE CROIX. via ARQUES.
    Bivouac in field.

June 6th Sunday. — March from Bivouac to
    STRAZEELE via EBLINGHAM &
    BORRÉ. Distance say 15 miles.
    Weather very hot cloudless sky.

(10th Fd. C.R.E.)

March 6 a.m. reach Billet at farm 2.30 p.m. rate of marching about 2. m.p.h. a most trying day. 1 Hr. halt about on the way & numerous checks & halts at the tail of 35th Inf Bde Column. The infantry fell out in such numbers as to stop the march. The Co. reached its billets in good form with about 8 casualties, 2 of whom fainted away, 1 sprained ankle & remainder genuine cases of bad feet & 2 men recently out of hospital. The Co Dr not Smith on the march & use of water bottles is discouraged. For the last 3 months training cigarettes have been prohibited during halts.
The halts if made at definite clock hours by units would be much more use to the tail of the column & when marching with Infantry only it would still be possible to water & feed the horses.

June 7th Monday. (Continued on A.F. C. 2118).

Army Form C. 2118.

WAR DIARY
or
INTELLIGENCE SUMMARY.
(Erase heading not required.)

Date	Hour	Summary of Events and Information	Remarks and references to Appendices

G.H.Q. 7/7/16	—	Marched at 8 a.m. reached Camp km 4 pm about 15 miles. A very hot day & high wind. Walked 1½ the last km or more. The infantry 31st Bde. who are in advance on the right turn, 7 men were lost through heat exhaustion & 3 though accident. Ramadis rever's Camp.
		
		Equipment. The mens marching capacity (given [un]training physique) Riad is not bad) could be greatly increased by:
		
		    a) Giving to summer wear lighter undershirting.
		    b) By slightly altering the tunic equipment so that the much [ ] out Sam Brown [temparden] round [sleeves of uniform].
		    c) By issuing neck curtains on having a cap which does not touch the top of the head.
		
		The men are very thoroughly done at the end of a mile march & would not have kept up for lack of arrival. The above alterations would I believe have changed this.	

8/7/16	—	Another hot day. Water bad & scarce. no sleep in camp. Several amoeamba killed. Day spent in creating shelter arranging parity water supply, Camp sanitation relieving up the horse and to billets in hot weather.	

Army Form C. 2118.

70th 70 Coy R.E.

WAR DIARY
or
INTELLIGENCE SUMMARY.
(Erase heading not required.)

Instructions regarding War Diaries and Intelligence Summaries are contained in F. S. Regs., Part II. and the Staff Manual respectively. Title pages will be prepared in manuscript.

Place	Date	Hour	Summary of Events and Information	Remarks and references to Appendices
9th June		—	A Section 7 3th Lieut Stevens RE. letter our yesterday's reconnaissance of an extn. of system's trenches to complete the works also proposed & sent to CRE	
10th June			The above scheme then away from 7th Co just of the defences. Officer went round the construction on the Left Bank of the LYS in front of PONT DE NIEPPE with CE & CRE. General Capper & his men in accord. 2 huts were built to cover at proper plan at 1/1000.	
11th			The Company commenced work on this 50 ft length of breastwork trenches in dugouts as de Some de Blaurice near Le Trou Tilleuls.	
12th			Section work in trenches & laying up communication trenches.	
13th			Sunday — Divy preached — churchparade with Canadian 27th Div.	
14th			Then to OOSTHOVE Farm for attachment to Field Coy on 27th D.: 1st & 2nd S/M ZbC & 7th F.C. RE	
		8:30 am.	Officer Stevens started & 7 man N.C.O.'s to have 3 hours instruction of the front & support trenches of the 3rd Div. side arm with under officers.	
15th			Night work 8 pm — 4 am. Section 143 Ammn work 3 am — 11 am. Hours to cover the heart of the day should be used from new in PLOEGSTEERT WOOD defences. accompany shelf RE working parties afore improving	
			Night work continued by 143. Sec 274	
16th			Morning work continued by Sec 274, section return rather 9 am to go on night work longer.	

1577 Wt. W10791/1773 500,000 1/15 D. D. & L. A.D.S.S./Forms/C. 2118.

WAR DIARY or INTELLIGENCE SUMMARY

Army Form C. 2118

Instructions regarding War Diaries and Intelligence Summaries are contained in F. S. Regs., Part II. and the Staff Manual respectively. Title pages will be prepared in manuscript.

(Erase heading not required.)

To 2nd Army HQ RE

Place	Date	Hour	Summary of Events and Information	Remarks and references to Appendices
	16—		8 p.m. – 4 a.m. Secs 1 & 3. 1–2 a.m. all on night work. The time between change of reliefs on work. All Officers & men have thus been two works in company & throughout. The supervision has entailed between an average of 12 hours being spent in the billet during zero. The supervision has been justified by practical result.	
	17— Thursday		Work in the support trenches continued mostly at night. The first Canadian (2 Pioneer Coys) arrived.	
	18—		Night work continues.	
	19—		The detachment of 7th Co. to work in the front line with the 1st South Irish and 7 Co. the 2nd S.M. 23 Co. 42nd Div. in the Ploegsteert Section & the trenches come to an end.	
	20—		Ca. remains at OOSTHOVE FARM.	
	21— Sunday		Rest day.	
	22—		The Company artisans become commenced to work after last upon the new lateron ERQUINGHEM & PONT DE NIEPPE on left bank of LYS. Machine Gun Sections came to rates trees & dickens M.G. emplacement forward. * emplacement design with subaltern officer. Infantry working parties commence work at C.E. from a Coy HQ town & CE HQ are a the Pont section to draw and from stores.	
	23— 24—	rest	Work continued on same works with Infantry parties when available.	
	25—		C. Willis moved to DOUDOU farm. – Company artisans works.	
	26—		Extermination & parks on gifts line – to sketch. Co on Willis clearing drains.	
	27—		Sunday.	
	28— 3 July		Continuation of work – Company working with 3rd Inf. Bde. in reserve.	
	4— July		Sunday	
	3— 10—		Work upon Report Centre Agenstras R.E. Brigade – & sketches.	
	11—		Sunday	

Army Form C. 2118.

To 7th Army R.E.

WAR DIARY
or
INTELLIGENCE SUMMARY.
(Erase heading not required.)

Place	Date	Hour	Summary of Events and Information	Remarks and references to Appendices
	12th July - 14th		Work in Nissen huts, also at WEMAER GLIDE (7 Trees) Support first near LE TOUQUET. Instructing Infantry in bombs & bomb throwing. The Company works yards are thoroughly organised, houses & Steam Saws (Small, with cut 6" cut) & Employs 53 Civilian workmen. Outpost consists of Frames for Dug outs, Gabion frames to Revetments, Frames to Trenches, prefab to save entanglement & screens. Experiments with Rifle grenade ranges, loopholes, Covers to Bombs &c in progress. Wagons Bodies have been fitted to Both Pontoon & Trestle waggons. This is only form of Transport in Constantly in use to the dispatch Forming from of Body to these waggons stands undoubtedly be much more by much shorter attacks. The Company has made a "caravan" for the water supply in its area by adopted upon sinking 50 new wells (about 20 ft deep) as a preliminary measure. Skilled labor has been steadily for deepened to meet. Field Co, as Establishment is constantly found too small, a large number of men could be handled readily by the same Co. Staff. A large increase in trades "clerks" &c materially enlarge on scope of usefulness.	

1577 Wt. W10791/1773 500,000 1/15 D. D. & L. A.D.S.S./Forms/C. 2118.

WAR DIARY or INTELLIGENCE SUMMARY

Army Form C. 2118.

170th Coy R.E.

Place	Date	Hour	Summary of Events and Information	Remarks and references to Appendices
	15th		No 1 & 4 Sections over to ARMENTIERES to take up work in the right sector of Dvl line, held by the 36th (Ulster) Bde., just taken over from the 27th Dv., R.E. 2nd Wessex Co.	
	16th–17th		Sections getting into the new lines. The distribution of R.E. material to Infantry is not easily & equitably arranged. Wastage of goods in the trenches is great, it is necessary for R.E. to control this. R.E. time is taken up with these own work that their difficult close cooperation with the Infantry which is essential becomes of R.E. Sec Commanders cannot get to know their Inf units in their line afford the latter to look to them for help & assistance in a natural way. Work on Trench Support & the Bde tvks continued.	
			Surveyor	
	18th			
	19th–24th		The above work continued. Wells being Sank. C. yard manufacturing by civil labour. Trench Support reconstructed. The system of working Infantry ad about indents for all Trenches through Sec Commders & Bdes then indented from the R.E. Co yard. First will soon be arranged in respect of gas position. In this way a proper control will be exercised. Much will have the assistance of higher real advice in all the works. Mining, Ventilation & all such draw Mine own storm visible been to look after them. Each drawn Mine own storm rockets bombs have now & anything else is unlikely to be surepfriches in must will be drawn from R.E. Co. in bulk by the Infantry & districted where they them. The Co have carried out experiments with Rifle Grenade rifle ammunition & have produced a Range Table in report upon this experimental mounting. (2nd Army wrte up futher)	

Army Form C. 2118.

To 2nd Army HQ

WAR DIARY
or
INTELLIGENCE SUMMARY.
(Erase heading not required.)

Instructions regarding War Diaries and Intelligence Summaries are contained in F.S. Regs., Part II. and the Staff Manual respectively. Title pages will be prepared in manuscript.

Place	Date	Hour	Summary of Events and Information	Remarks and references to Appendices
	24th July (contd.)		A new pattern of Rifle Grenade has been found and reported upon. Experiments have been made to find a suitable way of carrying Bombs into action. The Stokenhot Specimens have not yet been inspected. Separate plate have been manufactured & experiment. The Steam Tramway in ARMENTIERES has been put into action then on difficulties. Marrying of joining the electric system of tramway gauge with the tramway line. The extremely sharp curves & the Trailer will not at present take the engines. Trolleys now serve as trucks the junction between the two will later time. The El Tramway generating station is being put into running order & will be given a trial run this week. The overhead conductors have all been broken down, it is not intended to use the tramway for this service.	
	25th Sunday		(The 2 section billed is in the El Tramway Station.)	
	26th 31st July		Work upon the defences of 36th HD (Reft.) Sector of the line were continued under the Brigadier with his section assisting in between. This was most found a satisfactory arrangement. The direction of the defences was taken over by CRE 14th D. - The bankers & guns in all 3 Brigade areas have been placed by the Co. August 1-31st. Two bridges (sm) & lock-gates gate have been prepared for demolition.	

1577 Wt. W10791/1773 500,000 1/15 D. D. & L. A.D.S.S./Forms/C. 2118.

Army Form C. 2118.

90th Coy RE

WAR DIARY
or
INTELLIGENCE SUMMARY.
(Erase heading not required.)

Place	Date	Hour	Summary of Events and Information	Remarks and references to Appendices
	Aug. 1-31		Work has been continued in Right Sector (36th & 52nd Divns) & Infantry Pioneers. Infantry working parties from 600 a day due reduct to about 4 to 3 days a week. One Co. of Pioneers has been continuously employed, working under our own Officers under R.E. Sec. Officers. As far as possible the men have been employed upon certain definite work, if a nature requiring greater skill than the infantry generally possess, such as wiring, revetting etc. This has proved quite successful & has been a means of expanding the capacity of the R.E. Companies to work. The infantry as a whole have been far below the standards of former laid down in the latest book. It may safely be asserted that none of the front line working parties have been sent in any 30 per Coy so fit unto in 2 & 4 th which although the ground is very easy digging. This cannot only possibly be found to account for this, all that the men have been overworked & their inferior training too little effect by the officers of the new Army.	

1577 Wt. W10791/1773 500,000 1/15 D. D. & L. A.D.S.S./Forms/C. 2118.

CRE n° 9 — Portable Searchlights.
Ref. G.300/3rd June 1906.

1) The searchlight equipment of this Coy has not been used to its fullest ext.

May I also be informed please that it is desired to carry over the light + carry out some trials first in the neighbourhood of this billet, + may I the informed where between what dates this can be done.

I presume that other units will have to be consulted.

2) Without making any further experiments it seems that the lights are not powerful enough to be used for back from the front line, + they will therefore be quickly shot away in their present form as there are only two.

Cld. 12th Sept. Ref. your E.442
Water for Evins Farm

As the mobilization equipment comprises no tools for this work and they are not able to be obtained except by special authority I am unable to say when or whether this work can be completed.

As regards the stores necessary I believe they are coming from the R.E. Park but I am unable to say when they will arrive.

It is suggested that representation be made with a view to obtaining authority for R.E. Parks to hold a number of ordinary useful tools in stock for issue & return when finished with by R.E. Companies as required. A suitable list could be drawn up.

7 8/15

A Hebru Tewinjorth
O.C. 2/5th Vol Bn

and in no case would it seem that greater efficiency ought to be attained by two workshops with two staffs than with one good worn staff.

10.15 pm.
30/7/15

McKenna
Major [?]
O.C. 70th [?]

I would bring to your notice that every possible economy has been exercised here both in saving material in design & labour in construction. It is unlikely that a Brigade Workshop could reach this standard of efficiency.

I would urge that any carpenters & blacksmiths available for Brigade workshops be at once attached to me to work under the existing supervision. The smiths could already be usefully employed (there remains always a shortage of this trade) & the carpenters could be employed as soon as more wood becomes available.

It would appear that this Company can be efficiently organised, if at full strength in officers, to meet all legitimate demands, given a large yard & enough material.

29/8/15

Dear Colonel,

As you mentioned the use the Co. workshops could be to the results a Company can produce upon a defence sector, the enclosed which is the output during 6 Wks will answer your question better than anything else I can say.

Besides this all pickets required for revetting & other purposes & all the woodwork for the wells has been produced by the Yard, as well as countless other miscellaneous items of woodwork.

Three men only have been taken from the Co. to assist the civilian labour. The possession of the Yard makes it possible to help oneself without being dependent upon the goodwill of other people.

It thus adds a great stimulus to be an efficient unit.

Sincerely yours,
Dickens

Col. 12th Div.   Ref. list (preliminary) of
                 tools, suggested for R.E. Park
                 to keep, promised to CE

A list is attached comprising
a rough enumeration of tools
required for R.E. work of various
descriptions which it is suggested
the R.E. Park ought to be ready to
supply & take back into store as
required by R.E. Companies on
demand.
No attempt has been made to
suggest the numbers or quantities
& it nor is the list to be considered
complete as if the principle be
conceded a far more careful
study of MODERN tools should be
made to include a sufficient number
of the best tools available for each
kind of work.
                              Jeffreys
                              Major RE
    21/8/15 —   O.C. XIIth Div R.E.

Coy. 12th Bn. Ref. CRR 889.
Brigade Workshops.

I would like to bring to your notice that as far as this Company is concerned & the Brigade area which it serves, the present conditions are as follow. —

1). The Company workshop is capable of turning out all the material required by the Brigade IF the raw material is available for manufacture.

The workshop has not by any means reached the limit of its output.

With the same staff for supervision it is capable of any further expansion required to meet the whole demands of the Brigade area.

At present only shortage of material prevents the workshop supplying all the manufactured articles which the Brigade can deal with each day.

22

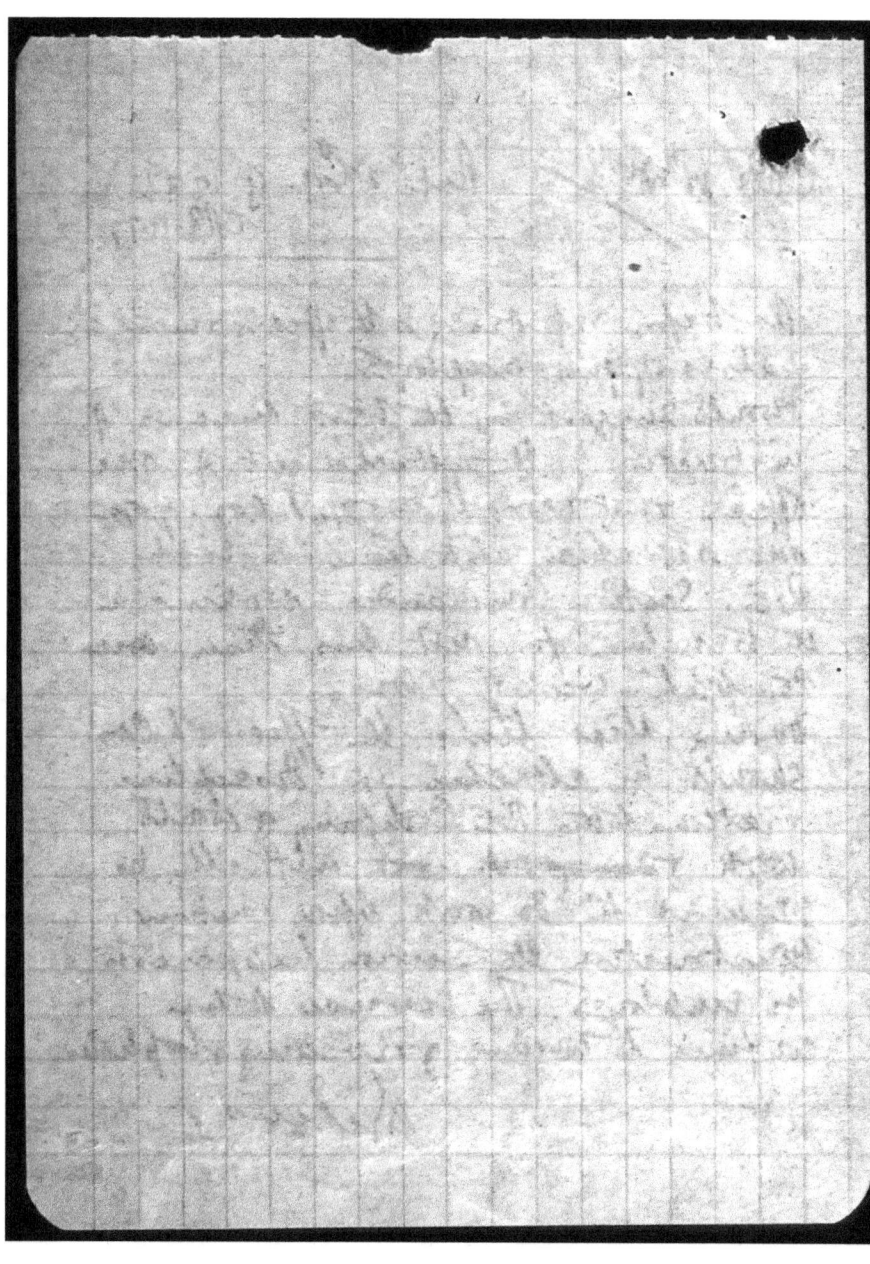

Trefsan Desyn 30/7/15. Brigade Workshops.

31/7/15 - Some of No 3 letter off 7 trees.
3/8/15 - Fixing bomb magazines constructed by C.B.
9/8/15 - Bombardment & repair of trench S9.
9/8/15 - Dugout Census.

10/8/15 - 111th Bde digging parties commence work on Subsid. Line.
12/8/15 - 7 Trees finished as bomb prof.   20/8/15

13/8/15 Commencement of dem. Ry bdge.

15/8/15 - Hastening completion of S trench.

17/8/15 - ? date of arrival of A Co. Pioneers
20/8/15 - Progress Rept.
20/8/15 - further hastening up completion of S. Trench.

22/8/15 - Commencement of Demolition scheme Ry bdge
2/9/15 - 7 Trees support finished plans sent in.
7/9/15 - O.C moves to A.

9th - last work on Subsidiary Line closed down.
17th - leave for Co. commences.

Army Form C. 2118.

12 Div

WAR DIARY
or
INTELLIGENCE SUMMARY.
(Erase heading not required.)

Instructions regarding War Diaries and Intelligence Summaries are contained in F. S. Regs., Part II. and the Staff Manual respectively. Title pages will be prepared in manuscript.

Place	Date	Hour	Summary of Events and Information	Remarks and references to Appendices
	Sept 25th	4.0 a.m.	Sections go to each stations in 36th AA Defence Sector HOUPLINES. War Sec, DOUDOU + 2 Sec ARMENTIERES + 2 Sec HOUPLINES. No working party after this hour.	
	26th		36th AR relieved by 151st AR. 58th Div at 6pm. 70th G Remains.	
	27th		Proper to Camp. Defences with 58th Div & hand on to 58th 58th Div War Sigt RE. Other sections to be informed & move by 9 pm. Standing by concentrating Section at ARMENTIERES.	
	28th		6 am march to TAILLY. Onwards were 1000pm beyond, dismounted by train from STEENWERCK & CHOCQUES. The onwards arriving at 11.30 pm in Stage of am after going for 17½ hrs covering about 30 miles to Chemin Ban, steff depair to show billets were march to VERQUIGNEUL KNIGHTS.	
	29th		March to Bivouac ½ mile W of VERMELLES. Took our French from 2nd Gp Brigade + 75th Field R. Brigade accounts at fifteenth then taking over.	
	30th		Reach bivouac 8.30 pm outside SH 4.30 pm all road blocks with traffic going both ways. Very overnight.	

WAR DIARY or INTELLIGENCE SUMMARY

Army Form C. 2118

Place	Date	Hour	Summary of Events and Information	Remarks and references to Appendices
	Oct	1st	Officer reconnoitre new line for front trenches running from 36.c.N.W. G.18.B.10.a. in front of Emery's registration at AUCHY on covering patrol. The Major moving traverse of Windmill bridge employed & sunk trenches released to form a fire screen. Pontoon trestles and striking shelter to columbine. The advance of the permanent bridges on Gerdonnellette and new trench held over approach.	
		2nd	Working Parties: - 430 men from the frontline trenches, 398 Pioneers, 600 from 16th in reserve, digging Assembly trench from G.18.13.10.1 to G.14.B.10.0 about 1000 yds + communication trenches to new Every important breech on road 200 yds to the front. Field guns kept up shrapnel fire all night on the enemy communication trenches. Pars of threads in front. They were unable to shell the road for fear of hurting our advancing party. 150 yds on the our side of enemy trenches to the road were cut there by the Suburban Spiers and new aeroplane gun proved over aware by the Suburban Spiers a the 16th in reserve got very hampered for inspite of having red flares a van silent extract.	
		3rd	Similar working parties again continued their day & day communication trench to 600 men from 26.c.N.W.G.17.D.5 9 to G.18.C.9.35. The parties were put in charge of 2nd in command s the myths work was much more satisfactory. When an advance was looked for them in connection charge of the work ± they get them position for they gas would. Officers transport Officers previously. The aver. of hygiene to be night our next events 20-25 ft in friable chalk/min.	
		4th	1st Continue working, employed on emergency patrol. 16th in reserve fail to man the entrenchments.	
		5th	Officer section taking morning knife in brigade, are covering patrol. Continue constructing T trenches in front of assembly trench.	

WAR DIARY or INTELLIGENCE SUMMARY

Army Form C. 2118

Place	Date	Hour	Summary of Events and Information	Remarks and references to Appendices
	Oct 5th		patrols fixed tramway in working order. Enemy had a complete control line all along town of Vermelles. Support trench in top of ground. This is being connected towards a 7am on line running parallel from VERMELLES.	
	Oct 6th		1 Sec. on Tramway (Daylight work) at Vermelles, 1 Sec. on Dugouts for Army Adm. wireless at "Bois Carré" 2.G. on Tramway (night work) in 2S German line.	Q. 6 S/
	Nov 7th		Tramway completed from dugout line back to German support line just behind VERMELLES. Co. to wide reserve for but remain billeted behind VERMELLES.	2 7/15

Pieces of Casualties to date →

N.C.O.					MEN.			
14/558	Sergt. James W.	S	12/9/15		52317	Sapper Page T.	S	3/9/15
4/2339	2/Cpl. Paget E.	W	1/9/15		4/1053	Sapper Simon E.	W	16/6/15
4/1493	Cpl. Hamm A.	W	3/9/15		6/0467	Driver Mercer T.	S	18/6/15
4/1500	L/Cpl. Langrick	W	3/9/15		4/2278	Sapper Slyde J.	W	24/6/15
4/0873	L/Cpl. Saunders W.	W	14/9/15		4/2689	Sapper Hesketh W.	S	29/6/15
					4/2081	Sapper Radley J.K.	K	21/7/15
					4/1913	" Tansley Rev.	W	20/9/15
					4/5080	" Springett W.	W	4/9/15
					6/1557	Pioneer Butler J.	W	15/9/15

S = Sick
W = Wounded
K = Killed

70th Coy RE

Army Form C. 2118

WAR DIARY
or
INTELLIGENCE SUMMARY.
(Erase heading not required.)

Instructions regarding War Diaries and Intelligence Summaries are contained in F.S. Regs., Part II. and the Staff Manual respectively. Title pages will be prepared in manuscript.

Place	Date	Hour	Summary of Events and Information	Remarks and references to Appendices
	Oct 8th to Oct 11th		Company in Reserve. Employed on wireless Inschallsen. Making up forward advance Dumps. Repairing tramway etc. Company work — 36th Inf. Regt.	
	Oct 12th		Moved billets to PHILOSOPHE	
	Oct 13th to Oct 17th		Company still in Reserve. Commenced a completed Support point at junction HURRICK ROAD and old German line. Placed water tanks with portable at several points. Commenced Trench in rear of front line from COERON AVENUE to St ELIE AVENUE. Assisted repair of GERMAN COMN. TRENCH now line in use. vide Report LXIVE attached.	
	Oct 18th		Continued Consolidation of Captured trench. N. harm been done in dusy the day.	Dug out N. of water Tower
	Oct 19th		Repair St FINE AVENUE & completion S.F.T. at junction St ELIE AVENUE.	35th Inf Regt
	Oct 20th Oct 21		Supports front line — fire step of COERON AVENUE to St ELIE AVENUE	
	Oct 22 to Oct 25		Reserve at FOUQUIERES. 3 New 2/Lts joined, vj. BETHELL, CATOR & DUKE. 6 months East Woolwich & Chatham. A valuable addition.	
	Oct 26		Aprised in a Company shoot on march out from PHILOSOPHE	
	Oct 27		Took over line KAISERIN TRENCH — HOHENZOLLERN REDOUBT — NEW TRENCH — AUCHY RAILWAY. Continued work Commenced 5.5th (Grants Knights) on 7 Saps parallels. Commenced CT led from H.R to old British line & Reg. S.F.T. 15 forward trench when Guildford and NEW TRENCHES. Started Dig-out old British line. Also 2 Mortar Trk. Wells and 6 New Bomb Dug-out Which and West of Railway. Working with 37th Inf. Regt.	
	Oct 28 29 30		Continued work Commenced on 27th & completed 2 CT's to NEW FORMED TRENCH. Some wiring done in front LITTLE WILLIE but stopped by report of Cos 36th Inf. Regt.	

20.10.15

C.R.E. 12th Div'n

I submit the following Report on the part taken by this Company in the capture of the German trench G6 c ½, 2. to G 12 A 2, 8½. on the night 18/19th October 1915.

The Assault was ordered to take place at 5.30. p.m. and orders were to capture the trench down to point G 12 A 2, 8.

OC Company Major BEHRENS RE ordered no 2 Section under LIEUT DUGGAN RE to be in position at point 90 at 5.30 pm ready to follow up the assault and consolidate the trench when captured. No 1 Section were ordered to be in reserve with the same object and at the same point under Capt: HAMILTON RE (the writer) at 6.30. pm. While No 4 Section was detailed to be ready at 10. pm. to dig a communication trench with a working Party from 35th INF BRIGADE from G 11 B. 9,5. to G 12 A 2, 8½. provided that the German trench had been captured. This Section was under Lieut DUNLOP RE.

I arrived at point 90 at 5.45. pm to find the assault had been postponed. Lieut DUNLOP accompanied me as he did not know the ground in which the communication trench was to be dug

2

as I intended to show it to him before 10 p.m. as time permitted. Having placed the reserve section (No 1) in the newly dug support trench G 11 B 7,5. to G 5 C 1,1. on each side of ST ELIE AVENUE so as to be well clear of Bombs Bomb-throwers machine gunners etc etc passing along the Avenue I proceeded to remain at point 90 till the Assault commenced and until 6.30. pm as ordered. The Assault commenced about 6.10. pm the Sappers (No 2 section) having previously taken up a position just in rear of the Bombers under cover of the already captured portion of the German head Parapet & in the dead ground in front and just South East of point 90. The officer with Bombers, LIEUT WALTERS, was wounded very early in the assault and I gave LIEUT DUGGAN permission at his request to take charge of and direct the assault of the bombers provided no infantry officer was present to do so.
This LIEUT DUGGAN did.
Arrived at the old barrier (No 1 subsection, consisting of Cpl Robins, and Sappers Whitelaw, Burrows, and Callaghan (by way) of the German parapet jumped down into the trench and proceeded to demolish the barrier to allow the bombers to pass and having completed this then proceeded on up the trench along which the Germans

~~was unsuccessful~~, followed by LIEUT DUGGAN along the West side of the trench until the remainder of the Sappers & all the Bombers, had already retreated. Bombers had also followed down the German trench.

This subsection (No 1) then came to a point G.12.A.2,8½ where they found men commencing to build a barrier which they continued to assist until practically all the bombers were killed or wounded, and it became necessary, in the absence of re-inforcements for them to hold the half built barrier by throwing Bombs themselves which they continued to do, assisted by the 4 or 5 Bombers still remaining alive for upwards of three-quarters of an hour until fresh Bombers came up. In this Sappers WHITELAW and BURROWS took the chief part and showed the greatest gallantry. Meanwhile LIEUT DUGGAN continued to direct the assault and also to superintend the placing of the remainder of his men for consolidation and saw that stores required were brought up as necessary.
A few minutes later word was passed back for the reserve section which I proceeded to return and bring up, and took charge of the consolidation of the newly captured trench.

A parapet was built, fire step provided, traverses constructed, trench deepened in some

4

...cers and raised in place, a second barrier with commanding loophole was raised, while extra accommodation in the form of scarps at the barrier head was provided for bombers and a machine gun emplacement undertaken.

The foundation for the parapet was a low bank of loose chalk and present a great amount of work in all of which the Infantry took a very real part and worked both by themselves and assisting the Sappers throughout the night with the greatest energy. In this Cpl ROBINSON RE was conspicuous for his encouragement and direction.

I now return to the period just after the assault had commenced when Major BEHRENS ordered LIEUT DUNLOP to go up and assist LIEUT DUGGAN consolidating in front and to remain there while he himself (Major BEHRENS) went back to take charge of the working party to arrange for the Communication trench from G 11 B 9.5. to G 11 A 2, 8½.

The night was bright moonlight and the ground over which it was intended to dig this trench was commanded by enemy machine gun fire from the ledge of the quarry at G 11 A 2½, 7½ and it is stated by those present that there was

was a sniper active in close proximity. Major BEHRENS made two attempts to lay out the trench with a tape ready for the working party.

At the first S/o CROSS was shot dead and at the second S/o GEE while Major BEHRENS was himself wounded.

This I did not learn until returning before dawn on the morning of the 19th. I found Major BEHRENS being taken into the Field Dressing Station at G 11 B 5.2.

Meanwhile Bombing continued almost continuous throughout the night the bombers all displaying the greatest gallantry & activity.

Early in the evening Lieut DUNLOP was wounded by a shell and had to be taken back while Lieut DUGGAN received a slight wound in the neck when leading the escalading party. This he had bound up but refused to give up his post.

Unfortunately this Officer was seriously wounded later. About 12 midnight Lieut SMITH reported to me that he had seen bombers outside the trench in an exposed position and as I did not consider the occasion at that period demanded any undue exposure I thought they should be brought into the trench. Lieut SMITH proceeded out to call

those were hit but he remained out as action
suddenly became imminent. Later he was
killed by a shell while still out and
Lieut DUGGAN went out to see whether
he was wounded or killed and if the
former to bring him in. Lieut SMITH
was it is regretted found dead and
Lieut DUGGAN himself received shrapnel
wounds in his stomach.

I have left the work for a short period
while I carried Lieut DUGGAN out over
the parapet through the dead ground
to point 90 as I wished to get him
back and his wound dressed as quickly
as possible.

I cannot speak too highly of the services of
Lieut DUGGAN throughout and they are well
deserving of recognition. To this I must
add the name of Sapper WHITELAW while
as aforementioned Cpl ROBINSON, and
Sappers BURROWS, CALLAGHAN & ROBINS
acted with great initiative and devotion to
duty.

Before closing this account I should like
to mention the care and close attention
to every detail given by Captain WATTS
of the ESSEX REGT to every portion of the
captured trench and its consolidation and

defence throughout the night.
The Bombers also deserve special mention
and though I do not know their names
I saw many work till they were either
killed or wounded some & continuing to
throw bombs for 3 or more hours while
one Lce Cpl of the ESSEX REGT particularly
distinguished himself from the ability
with which he directed bombing operations
where no officer was present.

Let me close with a further mention of
those who with one and all worked to
perform the duty entrusted to them —

Names of those mentioned (R.E only).
order of merit

(2.) Major. T. T. BEHRENS. R.E (wounded)
(1.) Lieut HERRICK. S. DUGGAN RE (wounded)
(3) No 4082 2/Corporal THOMAS ROBINSON
(5) No 59692 L.ce Cpl ERMEST ROBINS
(6) No 42021 Sapper GEORGE BLAND
(4) No 45098 " JOSEPH GALLAGHAN
(2) No 41929 " WILLIAM BURROWS
(1.) No 61510 " JOHN WHITELAW

Sapper BLAND is mentioned as having been the first to
jump up under heavy machine gun fire & wounded those at the parapet also
had undertaken work at my direction.

Jack Rudie N Pendleton
Captain R.E
O.C. 170th Coy R.E.
20.10.15

70th P.C.R.E.
Vol: 2

7984/14

70th Field Coy R.E.

WAR DIARY

for

November & December

1915.

Army Form C. 2118.

WAR DIARY
or
INTELLIGENCE SUMMARY.

70th Tunn. Co. R.E.

(Erase heading not required.)

Place	Date	Hour	Summary of Events and Information	Remarks and references to Appendices
	November 1915			
	1st 13th		Continued work opposite Little WILLIE and in the HOHENZOLLERN REDOUBT on Saps, Dug outs, Machine Gun Emplacements and general improvement of trenches. Practically no work has been done in improvement and protection of the roofs in the ace dug outs. Summer in the trenches were either jujiles, or jumping into S.Bs. The C.T. R.E. Carsequest knee deep in mud and external affairs to show it despair. Much work has been done by R.E. & Pioneers in making or laying trench boards. The Engineer Coys who shared the line on Nov 27 - Oct. and the works already with shift the 36th and 37th Infantry Brigades. During UCY have STICKY TRENCH and MUD TRENCH have been completed — UCZ tunnel & Sapping and NORTHAMPTON TRENCH (5 FT.) QUARRY ROAD, LEFT BOYAU, RIGHT BOYAU and a NEW CORK STREET all East of the old British Line have been dug — 40 dumps put down and captured which proves very effective against shrapnel but e direct hits on one partly demolished — 2 bomb hits were not serious — a new double rope front stone constructed — and 2 aid posts & dressing stations, and a dug in Forward Communal trench made. One hut no less than 12 different Saps are in hand of some description.	
	14th 15	6 am 15 30	The Coy. marched 15 K.Ss from St ANNEZIN, & did not accompany the Divn to LILLERS. The Coy marched 2 days from this line N. but it was billeted an order including the flowing g 2 hours. From the 17th Nov. and afterwards it paraded daily Sunday included at 6 am and worked till dark. During this time a Div school — a Div Laundry and a Div Recreation Room were established from existing buildings and a Dye Carp. already built up. Things including Class Room Bath Rooms Three Tennis Drying Rooms Cutters Band etc with complete Electric lights - and water R.H.S. joined the Coy on the 17th. — Baker, Norman Captn R.E. O/C 70 K.E.	A toucher our staff is attached

Marching Out State for 70th Fd Coy RE
from ANNEQUIN   14.11.15.

Section		Number	Remarks
Section I.	Dismounted	34 + 1 officer	
	Mounted	6	
Section II.	Dismounted	31 + 1 officer	
	Mounted	6	
Section III	Dismounted	32 + 1 officer	
	Mounted	6	
Section IV	Dismounted	35 + 1 officer	
	Mounted	6	
Headquarters	Dismounted	15 + 1 officer	2 attached A.S.C.
	Mounted	29	not included

Total   5 Officers   200 other Ranks.

WAR DIARY

Army Form C. 2118.

INTELLIGENCE SUMMARY. — 70th Field Coy RE

(Erase heading not required.)

Place	Date	Hour	Summary of Events and Information	Remarks and references to Appendices
	December 1915			
	1st to 4th		The Company continued work on the Div. Officers Quarters, Laundry, and Recreation Room and made many carrying and small alterations for many of various things in the S.W. side. It was attached temporarily V/LCT CRE 33rd Div. Relief arrived in France and worked with a Company of Pioneers on SHETLAND ROAD, a C.T. not East of Festubert, running. It with hurdles and layers 2'6" to 3'6" in depth. 200 yards of this were completed, but the work could not be continued at night when the Div. and the Company moved to the line the 11th – and the work carried out had been very heavy – it was very below line. It was unfortunate as available to the Continuous in rear of the new line most urgently required while the line was unfortunately but available to the Continuous in rear.	
	5th 6th 7th 8th 9th 10th			
	11th		The Company moved up to GORRE & were billeted in GORRE BREWERY. A month not state is attached. The billets consist of ANNEZIN — chiefly due to our Lieutenant is at the BREWERY on left of the most complete not Annezin to Lillers — and those of France	
	12th 13th 14th 15th 16th 17th 18th 19th		Corps on the Reserve line here. The Company was placed in Reserve the Reserve line by here is to all ground back of the SUEZ CANAL which the B.Y. and by th. This is not places in the front line and the left and Right Brigades Respectively. The whole Company ordered on Company of Pioneers was immediately detailed to drain the Divis. area West the SUEZ CANAL which are considering the length of time it has respective little drainage with apparent is have been done, and in the large of the very careful examination the hutes was not to drop 18 inches	
	20th		and the Employment after while Company became numerous from the 20th down the Village Line Defences — RUE d'EPINETTE — RUE CAILLOUX	

WAR DIARY

INTELLIGENCE SUMMARY.

7th Bn: CoY R.C.

December 1915

20th to 31st

FESTUBERT — LE PLANTIN — WINDY CORNER — Because of full infantry, the Bn. includes Machine Gun Replacements and was - one of this purpose 2 sections of M.G. 2/12 R.G.A. were attached for that to form the 23rd Div. O/L's & work out their little line. It & shew much progress. A. 15 Gun Proj. Replacement had been dropped and a section M.G. Company is to plant an its institution on 2 places - one period. It is hoped before the Company leaves the line, that the platoon of Pioneers is to plant on the main. Tired in land with this Observation Posts more than to them repair and replace the close return dugouts while a certain am. of Dug. Rooms, Gun stones, etc are beginning to send Bats in the front line to the Village line. Dugouts for each Bat's advice on the erection of gun replacement. The Company also sprayed assistance and in addition CHESHIRE ROAD and drainage has still to be maintained and it from length of repaired entries and slatting with hand loads thought it could easily 650 yards. A section of the Half F.C. have had to assist and supervise at Observation Posts. The Drys. Rooms, Gun Boot stones, Cheap Rooms, Quick Bat stores the at WINDY CORNER, LE PLANTIN SOUTH, RUE CAILLOUX, RUE DE L'EPINETTE are in the hands of a Sect section M.G. Company which looks after assurance M.G. Gunners & repairs to has huts An 18 pr. and a 6th: How: Battery M.G. Replacement as models. The 3 sections assists in 3 Platoons D & C Pioneers (6th Northants) to replace in CHESHIRE ROAD and drainage general works. The 4th Sect. M.G. Company is detached & works in the improvement of the other & billet in BETHUNE under the CRE. The above details the employment of the Company generally and it is hoped that space but infantries the greater part of the CoY.

A.D.S.S./Forms/C.2118.

Marching Out State of 70th F.C. Coy. R.E.
from ANNEZIN. 11.12.15

Section 2	Dismounted	35
Section 2	Mounted	6
Section 3	Dismounted	35
Section 3	Mounted	6
Section 4	Dismounted	34
Section 4	Mounted	6
Headquarters	Dismounted	17
Headquarters	Mounted	27

Cpl Crawford }
Dvr Nicholls } on Leave   166
Sapper Bodenham (C.R.E's Orderly)   3

Section 1. Left at ANNEZIN
  1 Officer
  Dismounted 34 (including Sapper Cawthorn on leave)
  Mounted 6.   } 40

Total Strength Company
including Section 1.   } 209 Other Ranks

To KPCRE.
Vol. 3
Jan '16

ORIGINAL

CONFIDENTIAL

— War Diary —
of
70th Field Company R.E.
from January 1, 1916 to January 31, 1916

WAR DIARY or INTELLIGENCE SUMMARY

Army Form C. 2118.

Place: **FESTUBERT** (Battle of Gorre Brewery)

Date: **1.1.16 to 18.1.16**

To 2nd Field Co. R.E.

January 1916

Date	Hour	Summary of Events and Information	Remarks and references to Appendices
1.1.16 to 18.1.16		The Company continued the work on the Reserve Line begun in December along the Village line RUE DE L'EPINETTE – RUE du CAILLOUX – FESTUBERT – LE PLANTIN – WINDY CORNER. No 2 Section with 3 Platoons of Queens continued making & siting CHESHIRE TRENCH which was completed (5th Notts.) the day before the D.V. went into rest – will reopen if some filling in. All went had to be done at night. No 3 Section undertook the erection of Drying Rooms at WINDY CORNER – LE PLANTIN – DANGER CORNER and set erecting of a Drying Room – Dry & Wet Gum Boot Stores – Changing Rooms – a Gulee Boot Store and a food message room. Space was allowed 600 gum boots & 1000 per Gulee boots at the same time as 4 Section undertook the erection of a M.G. Emplacement of 18" Ferroconcrete in the M. infrent? Village line in concrete and brick with the main Emplacement this comprised a 18" thick in the walls with air space of 12 inches formed by asbestos half 18" thick in the outside. The roof was formed of a double row of steel rods with 6" air space between in a steel frame. 2 Sections of the 2.12 ½ Co R.E. were attached to 2 Emplacement in stone emplacements but had not time to do more than the excavations to 2 Emplacements. One Emplacement eg No 13 at CAILLOUX POST was completed & a seat no 10 half finished. At the same time No 3 Section constructed 2 specimen Gun Emplacements to 6" Hows are 18 pr respectively – made by Carpenter of R.E. props and Sandbag built up on a wooden raft – with a roof of 9" × 3" corrugated iron East & broken bricks. Drawings of these were approved of and taken to all batteries in the Division. The Emplacements constructed had roofs of 12" earth & 8" brick & were shrapnel proof. Allowance was also made for a Scout & Sniper roof on each with a 12" inch air space – the Scout & his Sniper in separate to be pulled. All the O.P.'s in the D.V. were also taken	

1577 Wt.W10791/1773 500,000 1/15 D.D.&L. A.D.S.S./Forms/C.2118.

WAR DIARY
or
INTELLIGENCE SUMMARY: 70th Field Co. RE

Army Form C. 2118.

January 1916

Place	Date	Hour	Summary of Events and Information	Remarks and references to Appendices

1.1.16

No 1 Section the Company out work repair work & minor improvement was carried out. Demands of this nature evidently became too many - and 2 Senior NCOs 1/2 Sections of 1 Co RE were attached to work on OP's. A considerable amount of discussion took place as to whether Sapper's work on OP's, trench shelters, dug outs inside the existing houses - and while the was proceed 1 Senior Carpenter a front part of Drain Room similar to those names above at RUE de L'ERMETTE

All four Sets of Drain Room were completed by the 13th.
It was eventually decided that Brick turrets to OP's were erected out the Chateau de Sly - and watchtower very St SCHOOL HOUSE, BUTCHER'S SHOP, GIRLS SCHOOL & HOUSE No 39 all in FESTUBERT and at THE BREWERY & GUN HOUSE both at CAILLOUX.
The 3 Sections by no 1 Section of the 70th Co RE which had hitherto been employed in special work in respect of billets in BETHUNE & ISO 3 latter by 1/2 Hants A.T. Coy and have been brought up to the work, & ISO the 12" hole, 12" air space out

Designs have been drawn out & approved - some similar the square have between with an 18" wall (brick or concrete shafts) - a centre Room where old sisters being made with circular shafts - a castavates wh pavement lined by other companies - these have MG outside shafts then 2'9" wide or 18" wall ISO 12" air space out

On Ruta 18 mtr (brick conater shaft). This construction is much quicker than the Square type and they. The telephone room must also be brief apart - A Senior NCO in material is offerted - dependant on the height of the staff. the like shafts it Square type is more economic - and is also better in very exposed places But 18 the wall style English A.D.S.S./Forms/C.2118.
house is doubted a Front Room is much

18.1.16

Army Form C. 2118.

WAR DIARY
or
INTELLIGENCE SUMMARY.

(Erase heading not required.)

January 1916

Place	Date	Hour	Summary of Events and Information	Remarks and references to Appendices
BOURECQ	1.1.16 to 17.1.16		Most obvious work to round one Byklt has been completed left the line that Mujived concrete foundations in but had been completed and brickwork commenced while in the line a platoon NCO & Mortars also completed 1500 yards double apron fence were chosen along the village line front in conjunction with the liaison NCO H.C. Replacements.	
	18.1.16		The Coy has now back 15 Kot billets at BOURECQ.	
	19.1.16 to 15		While in rest much attention has been paid to drill – 3 day we spent Partroom out in practice with the wooden huts on the LA BASSÉE canal 3 days in learning out practicing a drive in the repair work: of high harbour wire Entanglement – at the end of the white day Col Seton ordered to 30 yards complete with 4 strand fence and to stand upon in front in 17 minutes while 2 day were spent in D.S. Maneuvers – practice in march discipline etc combined with a outpost scheme. A Semaphore Signal class is also in being and Santa behind drive is of frequent occurrence.	
	31.1.16		At the close NCo month the Company is sick in rest.	

Laurence Carmichael RE
[signature] O.C. RE

SECRET.

War Diary

for Month of February 1916

76th Field Company
Royal Engineers

29.2.16.

Army Form C. 2118.

WAR DIARY
or
INTELLIGENCE SUMMARY.

70th Field Coy RE

February 1916.

Place	Date	Hour	Summary of Events and Information	Remarks and references to Appendices
Bourecq & Philosophe	1.2.16 to 10.2.16		The Company continued in Rest billets at BOURECQ	
	11.2.16		The Company marched to PHILOSOPHE	
	12.2.16 to 29.2.16		The Company was allotted the portion of the line from MUD TRENCH (inclusive) LE ST ELIE AVENUE (exclusive) opposite the HOHENZOLLERN REDOUBT. Its area includes work on RESERVE TRENCH in rear. This is the part of the line in which the Company worked in October and November 1915. On that line trenches had not been bombed and the work had accumulated late. This has now been finished and the trenches are in much better condition. The old British line had been abandoned since then and communication trenches taken straight down from some of the old saps up — a great improvement. The line was taken over from the Dismounted Division who had suffered heavy casualties during their occupation. This had in part due to the fact that of dug-outs, none having been put in except 3 deep and by the main Cuspar saps. Since the Company left in November some light having then been constructed. This matter was considered to be all important and 2 Sellars have been constructed & Supplies on the work in Northampton and 47 VIGO Trenches and have been completed to accommodate amyth four men each. A 3rd Sellar has been continuously employed work continues to have relief through	

PHILOSOPHE

Army Form C. 2118.

WAR DIARY
or
INTELLIGENCE SUMMARY.

70th Field Coy RE

February 1916

(Erase heading not required.)

Place	Date	Hour	Summary of Events and Information	Remarks and references to Appendices
PHILOSOPHE	29.2.16 to 21.2.16		The work on Machine Gun Emplacements of the new rifle pit pattern & the German type with two entrances East have been practically completed. The 4th Shelter has been further altered. Dug outs shelter D while 26 has been completed, making Dug-outs to all Dug-outs shelter D while 26 has been completed, making Dug-outs to all Communication Trenches – Australian, Tit-head & Gordon Alley with improved (overhead) entrances, continuation of Machine Gun Emplacement, Machine Gun Dug-outs, and general repair and putting in order of the head. Some 1000 x 9 high wire entanglement have also been erected. The attached Company of the 5th Northants Pioneers. Has been also assisted in other of the above work and has responsible for the maintenance & upkeep of Communication Trenches between this and the Front line. During the above period the Company has worked with – both the 36th and 37th Infantry Brigades.	

Lawrence Naunton
Captain RE
OC 70th Field Coy RE
29.2.16

1912 to seies Vol. 5

March 31st 1916

Confidential

Original of
War Diary
of

70th Field Company Royal Engineers

From March 1st 1916 to March 31st 1916

Army Form C. 2118.

WAR DIARY
or
INTELLIGENCE SUMMARY

70th Field Coy - R.E.

March 1916

(Erase heading not required.)

Place	Date	Hour	Summary of Events and Information	Remarks and references to Appendices
	1.3.16 to 2.3.16		On the 26th February secret instructions were received that two mines would be exploded in the HOHENZOLLERN REDOUBT on the night of the 2nd March. The craters so formed would be occupied by the 36th I.B. with whom the Company was working, and at the same time an assault would be carried out on the CHORD. Preparations were immediately commenced. Owing to the proximity of the mines the assault on the CHORD could not take place from the HOGS BACK - but must be from WEST FACE. The HOGS BACK was accordingly bridged and ladders for the assault placed in WEST FACE. Fifteen special Bomb stores were constructed. Two special dumps for R.E. stores were made and material collected - one to the Northern & one to the Southernmost group of craters. Special attention was also given to Communications and to this purpose two Russian Saps were commenced towards the sites of the new craters to be occupied - one this Sap was 6 ft. in greatest width & the roof being easily broken down and thorough Communication very quickly established with the minimum number of Casualties. One row was supported with mine casing which went forward just before the mines were due to explode. Very complete orders were issued by the G.O.C 36th I.B. while those for R.E. and Pioneers were issued by me - a copy of which is attached. Unfortunately the assault on the Northern Half of the CHORD was not successful and this necessitated the abandonment of the opening up of the old Communication between HOGS BACK and the CHORD. Otherwise all arrangements were carried out without a hitch.	

Original

WAR DIARY
or
INTELLIGENCE SUMMARY.   70th Field Co - RE

March 1916

Army Form C. 2118.

Place	Date	Hour	Summary of Events and Information	Remarks and references to Appendices
PHILOSOPHE	2.3.16		The work of Consolidation of the Craters was carried on all through the night and a very great deal of work was done, while communication has been opened up. Together the whole system. Casualties, chiefly from shell fire were very heavy. Both Officers were wounded, 6 men were killed, 2 missing believed killed, and 13 men wounded. All behaved with the greatest coolness & devotion to duty — and it is important to speak highly of the work of the men. Today the 31st March telegrams have been received awarding the D.S.O. to the OC of the Company (Impey) and the M.C. to 2/Lieuts DUKE & JACKSON. Later rumours have been current of a new medal & ribbon to be awarded to men for good work performed. One cannot help feeling the want of such a medal specially for those employed in work as R.E. & Pioneers where opportunities in the award of the D.C.M. do not often present themselves, but where it is frequently evident that some reward is richly deserved. A copy of my report to the C.R.E. on the operations is attached.	
	3.3.16 to 6.3.16		Work on consolidation of the Craters was continued night & day. The Parados on the far lip was completed — many loopholes put in — a roadway constructed round the inside of each to behind the Parados — and a sandbag wall built up on the edge to form protection from shells bursting in the Craters. Deep Dug-outs were commenced, 4 in each Crater, sited below the new mine shafts commenced by the Miners, with heavy protective sandbag walls outside the entrances. All communications were deepened where necessary and the Whole thoroughly consolidated. Shelling was continuous during the period and the Company suffered further casualties.	

Army Form C. 2118.

WAR DIARY
or
INTELLIGENCE SUMMARY.

70th Field Co. R.E.

March 1916

(Erase heading not required.)

Place	Date	Hour	Summary of Events and Information	Remarks and references to Appendices
	7.3.16		The C.R.E. 12th Divn and the Medical Officer examined the Company shelter and work was recently handed over to the 69th and 87th G.S. R.E. - the former taking the Southern & the latter the Northernmost group of Craters. Have two Companies continued to improve the work of consolidation, the fan lip of the craters & also commenced consolidation of the rear lip.	
	7.3.16 to 11.3.16		The Company rested - and was drilled.	
	12.3.16		The Company took over work in the Right Brigade area from the 87th G.S. R.E. who had also continued to be responsible for this portion of the line. Officer Sketches has been employed in construction deep dug-outs shelters - One Section has constructed many dug-out shelters to men in the Support Fire Trench - While the fourth Section has completed the return line up to the O.G.1 - installed a new pump in O.B.4 which is very successful - Completed a new room to the Bgd H.Q. dug-out - constructed T heads in various places and done work in creating a loophole where necessary. Two Platoons "B" Co 15th Northants (Pioneers) have been employed in deep dug-outs while two have been engaged in maintenance of work of Company & C.T's and in assisting Infantry to make knife rests. During this period the Company has worked with the 36th & 37th Infantry Brigades.	
	31.3.16			

JaRuis Manulus
Captain R.E.
OC 70th Field Co. R.E.
31.3.16

PHILOSOPH

4.3.16.

C.R.E 12th D.Wⁿ

1. I submit the following report on the work of this Company during the Operations of 2nd/3rd March

2. Orders were carried in accordance with O.Oˢ issued, copy of which was submitted on 2nd moⁿᵗ

3. Detailed Instructions for consolidation were
(a) If craters were at a slope of over 45% to construct parapet as below:—

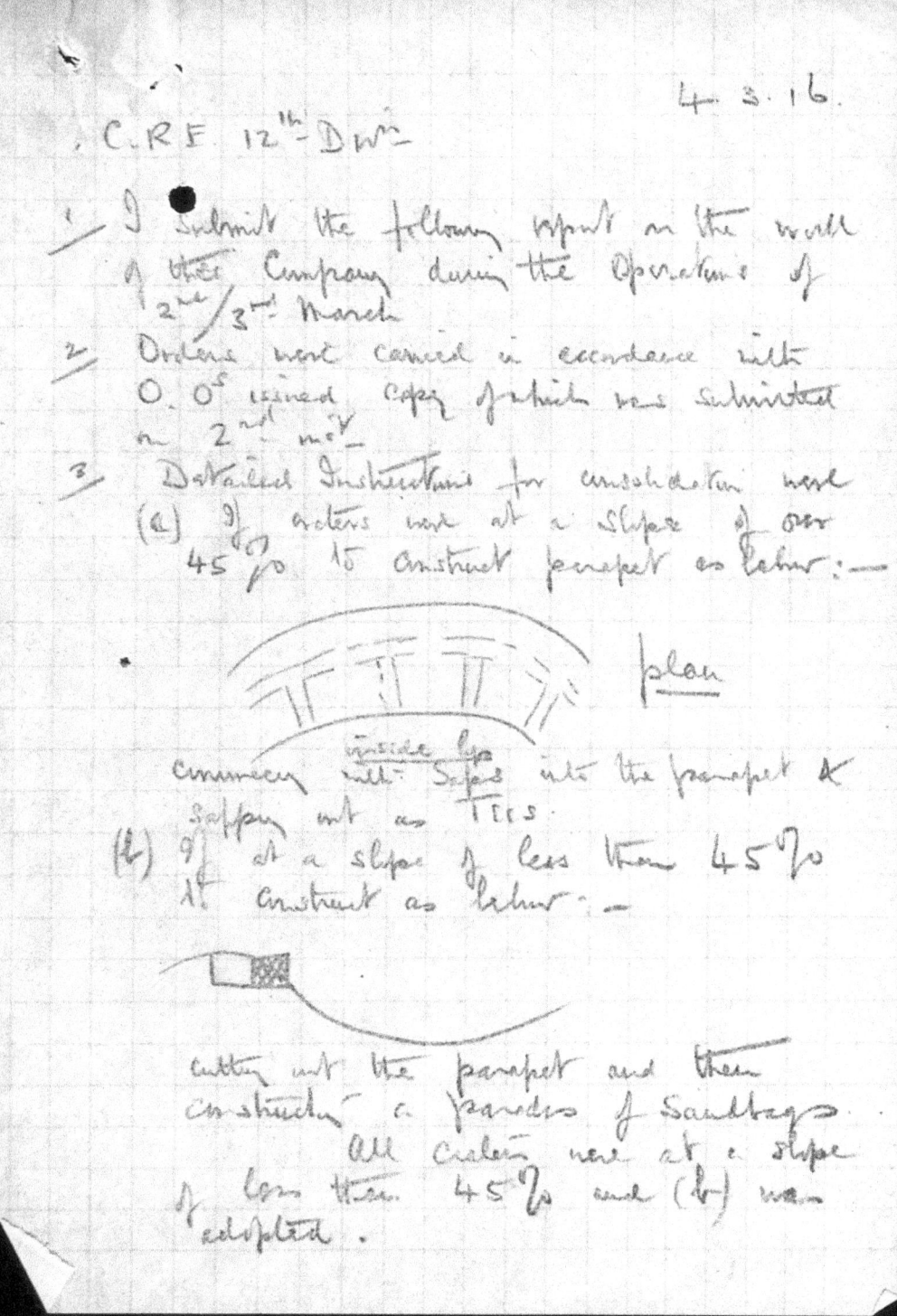

plan

connecting with saps into the parapet & sapping out as TEES.

(b) If at a slope of less than 45% to construct as below:—

cutting into the parapet and then constructing a parados of sandbags.
All craters were at a slope of less than 45% and (b) was adopted.

3/ In addition to above a shelter trench was to be dug in rear of the parados and as far up the slope of the crater as possible roofed over with corrugated iron if it could be got up, the trench being six feet deep and 18 inches wide.

This was done but could not be roofed over. Since then however slides have closed up nearly all these trenches and dug outs are being commenced going straight into the sides of the crater.

4/ Communication Trenches were commenced as in Op O² but that from HOOGE BACK to the CHORD had to be abandoned.

The Russian Saps proved most successful as far as they went and a C.T. 6 feet deep was quickly opened up in each case. Beyond however rifle and machine gun fire made progress difficult and the Pioneers did not succeed in carrying the trench more than one to one & a half feet deep.

Should time in the future be available

orders to return to the Dressing Station

a. Sergt ROBINSON. RE
This N.C.O displayed great coolness and initiative and carried on through the night until daybreak though Lieut DUKE had been wounded without further orders from me. His work was excellent

b. Actg Cpl E THOMAS. RE
This N.C.O displayed great coolness and resource through the night, being of the greatest assistance to 2/Lieut JACKSON RE after he was wounded and carrying on until he was relieved.
He stayed behind in the morning to bring back a wounded comrade from the crater and was unfortunately killed while trying to get him out by a sniper, being shot through the head

c. I cannot speak too highly of the courage and devotion to duty evinced by all men engaged.

Lieut [signature]
OC [signature]
4/3/16

SECRET.   Copy No 1

1st March 1916

70th Field Co. R.E. Operation Orders No 1.
by Captain S.W.S. Hamilton, R.E.

1st March 1916

Supplementary to 36th Inf. Bde. Operation Order No. 79 of 1.3.16.

2 Sections 70th Fd. Co. R.E. and 4 platoons 5th Northants Pioneers will be in advance. 1 section 70th Fd. Co. R.E. and 1 platoon Pioneers will be in Reserve.

Detail for R.E.

One half No. 2 Section (2 Lt. Jackson R.E.) will form up in GUILDFORD TRENCH in rear of party E appendix II, whose objective is Crater C. The head of the ½ section being fifty yards up GUILDFORD TRENCH from its junction with the O.B. line, and will be followed by a carrying party of 30 men vide g (App II).

The second half-section will form up in rear of the above, and will extend through the O.B. line down QUARRY ALLEY, followed by a second carrying party of 30 men, vide g (App II).

Immediately the party detailed to occupy Crater C has started they will move up to the Ramp in Sap 12 and there await messengers from Craters B & C that all resistance has ceased, when they will at once advance, the first half section and carrying party E to Crater B, the second half section and carrying party to Crater C, and commence consolidation of the position as per separate detailed instructions issued.

No 4 Section (2 Lt. Duke R.E.) will form up in SAVILE ROW in rear of party g (Appendix I), support for No 2 Crater, the head of the section being at the junction of SAVILE ROW & VIGO STREET, and will be followed by a carrying party of 30 men vide h (appI).

When all resistance has ceased, a guide will be sent to report to the officer in charge of Working Parties, and will guide both the above up to 'A' Crater, where they will at once commence consolidation of the position as per separate detailed instructions issued.

2.

This Section R.E. will also be in charge of Communication Trenches to be dug as below for which it will send back for additional Working Parties to those detailed in para 17 of O.O. No. 79, if required.
(a) from Crater A to the CHORD to the right of the Crater.
(b) from Crater A to Crater No. 2.
(c) from the junction of Crater A & Crater No 2 to Hog's Back.

The Officer in Charge of this Section will also be available for advice in consolidation of Craters Nos 1 & 2, and will assist as much as possible.

Detail for Pioneers.

Two platoons Pioneers will form up in QUARRY ALLEY in rear of No. 3 Section 70th Fd.Co. R.E. and of the carrying party of 30 men vide g (App II).
They will follow up GUILDFORD TRENCH as soon as parties in front have moved off and will halt at the junction of GUILDFORD and NORTHAMPTON TRENCH where they will await information as to all resistance having ceased.

Having received this information they will wait until it is sufficiently dark, when one platoon will proceed to break down the Russian Sap leading from STICKY TRENCH to Crater C. and to continue digging such portion as is not completed until it has joined up with and forms a communication with Crater C.

It will be assisted by 30 Infantry, 8th R.F, who will be obtained from the Officer in Charge of Working Parties at No 2 Dump.

The second platoon will wire in front of this new Communication Trench from STICKY to the N. edge of Crater C.

A third platoon will form up in VIGO TRENCH facing North, at the its head at the junction of VIGO TRENCH and SAVILE ROW MALCRIN TRENCH, and when sufficiently dark, will follow Party i (app1) up Savile Row, HOG'S BACK where it will proceed through No 3 Crater and open up the old Communication Trench that leads from there to the CHORD

It will be assisted by 50 Infantry (9th R.F.) who will be obtained from the Officer in Charge working Parties at No. 1. Dump.

The fourth platoon will form up in VIGO TRENCH in rear of the third, whom it will follow up SAVILE ROW and KAISERIN TRENCH to the Russian Sap leading to No. 1. Crater which it will proceed to break down and to continue digging such portion as is not completed until it has joined up with and forms a communication with Crater No. 1

Should it require assistance of an Infantry working Party it will apply to the Officer i/c W.P.s at No.1 Dump.

The three Communication trenches detailed above must be completed before dawn on the 3rd March at all costs Their importance cannot be over-estimated, and on them the eventual success of the whole operation will depend.

Where necessary, additional working parties will be indented for on the Officers in charge of W.P.s at Nos. 1 & 2 Dumps, according to the position of the C.T. for which they are required.

75% Shovels and 25% picks will be carried.

RESERVE No.1 Section 70th Fd.Co. R.E. (2/Lt Papworth R.E.) and one platoon of Pioneers will be held in reserve and will take up their positions in the O.B. Line at its junction with BART'S ALLEY – the R.E. on the South and the PIONEERS on the North Side. Should any portion of the RESERVE be necessary it will proceed along the O.B. Line and up via SAVILE ROW or LEFT BOYAU according to the position of the work for which it is required.

All Sections and platoons will be in the positions detailed by 5.15 p.m.

Position of O.C. R.E. & PIONEERS:—
The O.C. 70th Fd.Co. R.E. and the O.C. "A" Co. 5th Northants will be with the G.O.C. 36 Inf. Bde.

Issued at 11 pm

Sackville Mannell
Captain R.E.
O.C. 70th Field Co. R.E.

Copies to :-

No. 1. Office.
" 2. Hd Qrs 36th Inf. Bde.
" 3. C.R.E. 12th Division.
" 4. O.C. No.1. Section 70th Fd Co R.E.
" 5. " No 3 " " "
" 6. " No 4 " " "
" 7. " 5th Northants Pioneers.
" 8. " 8th Royal Fusiliers.
" 9. " 9th Royal Fusiliers.

ORIGINAL

App 70 FOR E
XII   Vol 6

Confidential

War Diary.

of

70th Field Company Royal Engineers

From April 1st 1916 to April 30th 1916

Volume 8.

WAR DIARY
or
INTELLIGENCE SUMMARY. 170th Field Coy RE

Army Form C. 2118.

April 1916

Place	Date	Hour	Summary of Events and Information	Remarks and references to Appendices
PHILOSOPHE	1.4.16 to 25.4.16		The Company continued to work alternately with the 37th – 35th – and 36th Infantry Brigade in the RIGHT (QUARRIES) SECTOR and was employed almost exclusively in building deep dug-outs for Machine Gunners and Staff in the Front & Support Line Trenches. Fourteen Dug-outs were completed for Machine Gunners & seven for Infantry. All were 16 feet below ground and & each had 2 Entrances. During the same period work was done in maintenance & repair of trench – in complete dog-leg and in opening up old trenches near headquarters. From 3 to 10 men employed almost nightly in work on craters back of the HAIRPIN & LOOKOUT CRESCENT. Men have been killed & wounded but on the whole casualties were few.	
HALT IRELUX	26.4.16 to 30.4.16		The Company was in Rest billets, and the days were spent in drill down the morning & keep games in the afternoon: during the past 24 months in the trenches has suffered many casualties.	

ORIGINAL

70 F CRE Vol 7

XII

War Diary

70th Field Coy RE

3rd Period

May 1st 1916 to 31st 1916.

Volume 9

WAR DIARY

Army Form C. 2118.

70th Field Company RE

May. 1916.

Place	Date	Hour	Summary of Events and Information	Remarks and references to Appendices
HAUT MEUX	1st to 20th		The Company continued in Rest Billets. The Daily Programme consisted of Physical Exercises, Rifle Exercises & Drill, a Musketry Course by Carroll at Cumerchy. The afternoons were chiefly devoted to Sports —	
MAZINGARBE	21st to 31st		The Company (less HQ) which remained at HAUT RIEUX moved to billets in MAZINGARBE and was attached to the 16th Division for work in the village line at the close MT units the Company in billets so attached. During the above period the Div. Monument at Rest.	
			The 70th Field Company R.E. was amongst the units specially mentioned in Sir Douglas Haig's despatch of May 1916 & has had her brought to his notice for special good work done the past six months.	

DeRins Ranson Captain RE
OC 76th Field Coy RE

70. FERE
vol 8
jeune

~~SECRET~~

Original

XII

War diary
70th Field Coy R.E.
1 Jany 1/16 — 30 6/16.

Volume 10

Army Form C. 2118.

WAR DIARY
or
INTELLIGENCE SUMMARY.

(Erase heading not required.)

June 1916 70th Field Co. R.E.

Instructions regarding War Diaries and Intelligence Summaries are contained in F. S. Regs., Part II. and the Staff Manual respectively. Title pages will be prepared in manuscript.

Place	Date	Hour	Summary of Events and Information	Remarks and references to Appendices
Mazingarbe	1/5-9/6	—	Coy. engaged on deep dugouts in Village line also M.G. emplacements wiring & fire trenches.	
	8/6	—	7 OR killed & 7 OR wounded in Mazingarbe	
	9/6	—	Coy moved to Hautereux (near Lillers) for rest.	
	9/6-16/6	—	Coy in rest at Hautereux.	
	17/6	—	Proceeded by rail & road via Amiens to Warquies.	
	16/6	—	Capt. T.D. Gemmill took over command of coy.	
	18/6-30/6	—	Coy in rest at Warquies.	
	22/6	—	Draft of 21 sappers recd from base.	

TDGemmill Capt RE
OC 70th Field Co RE.

30/6

12/ July
70 F.E.R.E
vol 9

ORIGINAL

WAR DIARY

70th FIELD COY R.E

Period

1.7.16 — 31.7.16

VOLUME 11

SECRET

Army Form C. 2118.

70th Field Coy RE WAR DIARY
12th Division
INTELLIGENCE SUMMARY July 1916
(Erase heading not required.)

Place	Date	Hour	Summary of Events and Information	Remarks and references to Appendices
Field	1.7.16	—	Coy moved from ST AMAND to Bruale.	
—"—	2.7.16	—	O.C. Coy, Lt. Papworth & Lieut. & 6 O.R. for section attached to 15th Co. RE at Orillers Post with a view to taking over from 15th Co. - 12th Div moved into the line.	
—"—	4.7.16	—	Remainder of Coy moved from Bruale to Orillers Post. Transport to Long Valley	
—"—	4.7.16			
—"—	5.7.16		Coy with attached infantry working parties, engaged by night in digging support line from our front line to S.W. corner of La Boiselle.	
—"—	6.7.16			
—"—	7.7.16		36th Bde. attack on OVILLERS.	
—"—	7.7.16		1 Sect. + attached inf. & pioneers attached to 76th Bde.	
—"—	8.7.16		2 Sect + attached Inf. + attached pioneers engaged on strong points in OVILLERS.	
—"—	9.7.16		Coy moved via ALBERT to VADENCOURT WOOD. 12th Div. withdrawn from the line.	
—"—	10.7.16		Coy resting in VADENCOURT WOOD.	
—"—	11.7.16		Coy moved from VADENCOURT WOOD to BUS-LES-ARTOIS	
—"—	12.7.16		Coy resting & refitting at BUS-LES-ARTOIS	
—"—	13.7.16 to		Coy employed on road making, drainage, fascine making for 2nd Water Supply points at OBUS & repairing trenches, taps etc. in connection therewith.	
—"—	20.7.16			
—"—	21.7.16		Coy moved from BUS-LES-ARTOIS to BERTRANCOURT — one section to MAILLY-MAILLET for work on reserve line.	
—"—	22.7.16		12th Div. moved into the line - 70th Co. in reserve.	
—"—	23.7.16		2 more sections moved to MAILLY MAILLET for work on	
—"—	26.7.16		3 sections withdrawn from MAILLY-MAILLET - 12th Div on leapfrog to & support line. withdrawn from the line.	
—"—	26.7.16		Coy moved from BERTRANCOURT to VARENNES.	
—"—	27.7.16		Coy moved from VARENNES to BOUZAINCOURT.	

1577 Wt.W10791/1773 500,000 1/15 D.D.&L. A.D.S.S./Forms/C. 2118.

70th Field Co. R.E.

WAR DIARY July 1916 (continued)

12th Div. INTELLIGENCE SUMMARY.

Army Form C. 2118.

Place	Date	Hour	Summary of Events and Information	Remarks and references to Appendices
Field	28.7.16	–	12th Div. moved into the line – 70th Co. RE in reserve – 3 sections moved to AVELUY for work on communication trenches, repairing old German dugouts, defences of OVILLERS – one section remains in BOUZAINCOURT for work on water supplies, baths, Divl. REYards etc. also HQrs Divn. of Corps & transport.	
–	29.7.16 to 31.7.16		Work as detailed above.	

J. G. Rumwila Capt RE
O.C. 70th Field Co RE

31/7/16

12/70/FE RE
Vol 18

War Diary (Original)
70th Field Coy R.E.

Volume 12

August 1st — 31st 1916

ORIGINAL

Army Form C. 2118.

70th Field Co. R.E. WAR DIARY 12th Division

INTELLIGENCE SUMMARY Aug 1916

Page 1

Place	Date	Hour	Summary of Events and Information	Remarks and references to Appendices
Bouzaincourt and Aveluy	1st/7th to 8th/8th		One section at Div. I. H.Q. Ors. for work in Div. I. Yard - water supply - engines etc. Three sections at Aveluy from work in & around Ovillers. Three sections on Commn. trenches, one section on 3 pumps of Ovillers & one section on repairing old Boche dugouts. Coy. in Div.l Reserve.	
	9/8/16		Section at Divl. H.Q. Ors. moves to Aveluy - 2 Sections attached to 69th Field Co. for work in the line.	
	9th to 13th		2 Sections in the line between Ovillers & Pozières - one section Commn. trenches 1½m Ovillers - one section defense of Ovillers.	
	14th–16th		3 sections in defense of Ovillers 1st Sec. commn. trenches than Ovillers 1st-5th July 70th severely wounded (Died in hospital at Heilly on 20th Aug).	
	13th		4 sections moves to Senlis	
	16th		Coy. moves to Authieulle	
	17th		Coy. moves to Simencourt	
	18th		Coy. in rest at Simencourt	
	19th–20th–21st		Inspection of 3 Field Cos. by G.O.C. 12th Div.	
	22nd		H.Qrs. & 3 sections moves to Wailly. 1 section to Agny.	
	23rd		Section officers & sergts. inspects line to be taken over in front of Agny.	
	24th		Half of each of Nos. 1, 3 & 4 Sections proceed to Agny.	
	26th		Remainder of No. 1, 3 & 4 Sections proceed to Agny - Relief of 67th Field Co. R.E. carried out - Coy. now attached to 36th Inf. Bde.	

Army Form C. 2118.

WAR DIARY
or
INTELLIGENCE SUMMARY.

(Erase heading not required.)

Place	Date	Hour	Summary of Events and Information	Remarks and references to Appendices
Agny	26th-31st		No. 3 Section work in left sector — No. 4 Section work in right sector of Bde. Area — No. 1 Section - refilling of Agny. No. 2 Section work in back area.	

J. Stewart Capt. R.E.
OC. 70th Field Coy. R.E.

31/8/16

Vol 4

ORIGINAL

WAR DIARY.
70th Field Coy R.E.
In France.
Sep. 1st 1916 — Sep. 30th 1916.

Volume. 13

SECRET

Army Form C. 2118.

70th Field Co. R.E. WAR DIARY 12th Div.

INTELLIGENCE SUMMARY.

(Erase heading not required.)

Instructions regarding War Diaries and Intelligence Summaries are contained in F. S. Regs., Part II. and the Staff Manual respectively. Title pages will be prepared in manuscript.

Place	Date	Hour	Summary of Events and Information	Remarks and references to Appendices
Agny	1st to 26th		Nos. 1, 3, & 4 Sections attached to 36th Inf. Bde holding G.S. sector (south of Arras), work consisting of trench maintenance, heavy, medium & light trench mortar emplacements, Russian Saps, dugouts, defences of and improvements to billets in Agny, covered saps or communication trenches etc. No. 2 Section employed under CRE in back area on baths, supply huts etc.	
	2nd - 20th		Lt. Fleming F.W. joined Coy from base.	
			Capt. F.T. Lee Norman appointed Adjt. to 12th Divisional Engineer.	
Warlus	26th		Nos. 1, 3, & 4 Sections Col-Brown from Agny to Warlus.	
Milly	27th		Coy proceeded by bus & road from Warlus to Milly (near Doullens)	
	28th		Coy transport proceeded from Milly to Talmas	
			Lt. Cator E.P.D transferred to 69th Fld Co & Lt. R. Kedou joined Coy from 69th Co. as recruits in Command.	
	29th		Coy proceeded from Milly to Pommier Redoubt (near Mametz) Transport from Talmas to Pommier Redoubt	

Bennett Capt. R.E.
O.C. 70th Co. R.E.
30/6

Vol 1·2

War Diary.

70th Field Coy R.E.
In France.

October 1st 1916 — Oct 31st 1916.

Volume 14.

SECRET

ORIGINAL SECRET
Army Form C. 2118.

70th Field Co. RE   12th Div.   Oct '16

WAR DIARY
INTELLIGENCE SUMMARY.
(Erase heading not required.)

Instructions regarding War Diaries and Intelligence Summaries are contained in F. S. Regs., Part II. and the Staff Manual respectively. Title pages will be prepared in manuscript.

Place	Date	Hour	Summary of Events and Information	Remarks and references to Appendices
Field	1.10.16		Coy. at POMMIERS REDOUBT (near MAMETZ) in rest.	
-"-	2.10.16		Coy. moved to camp near BERNAFAY WOOD - 12th Div. now in the line near GUEDECOURT. Work commenced on repairs to LONGUEVAL-FLERS road under CRE's orders	
-"-	2nd to 8th		Coy. employed, mostly by night, on repairs to LONGUEVAL-FLERS road and Decauville railways in & about LONGUEVAL, from thence to FLERS, with special items as follows:- 3 sections attached to 36th Inf. Bde. for operations. Sections not employed owing to failure of attack.	
-"-	9/8			
-"-	12/13		4 Sections attached to 35th Inf. Bde. for operations. Owing to failure of attack, coy. employed wiring front line	
-"-	13th/14th		2 Sections attached to 35th Inf. Bde. for work on coy. dugouts, & superintendence of Inf. parties employed in clearing old & digging new trenches.	
-"-	17/18		attack by 35th Inf. Bde. - 2 Sections attached for operations - Owing to failure of attack, one section was not employed. Remaining section employed in supplying forward	
-"-	18/19		a new tramed towards Boole. One section attached for operations to 35th Inf. Bde. - (attack cancelled)	
-"-	20th		Coy. moved to camp near MONTAUBAN & came under orders of C.R.E. XV Corps troops - 12th Div. retiring from the line.	
-"-	21st to 31st		Coy. employed under C.R.E. XV Corps Troops erecting Nissen huts in new Brigade dump near MONTAUBAN.	

Stennell Capt RE
O.C. 70th Co. R.E.

31/10/16

Vol 13.

WAR DIARY

"70th FIELD COMPANY R.E

for period
Nov. 1st 1916 – Nov. 30th 1916

VOLUME 15

SECRET

ORIGINAL

Army Form C. 2118.

SECRET

WAR DIARY
70th Field Co. RE   12th Div.

INTELLIGENCE SUMMARY.
(Erase heading not required.)

Nov. 16.

Place	Date	Hour	Summary of Events and Information	Remarks and references to Appendices
Field	30/10	—	Coy. moved from near MONTAUBAN to near DERNANCOURT.	
"	31/10	—	Transport & cyclists proceeded from near DERNANCOURT to TALMAS	
"	1/11	—	" " TALMAS to MILLY (near DOULLENS).	
			Dismounted portion of coy. by train to GOUY-EN-ARTOIS. Transport moved from MILLY to GOUY where Coy. again came under orders of CRE 12th Div.	
"	2/11	—	Coy. in rest at GOUY.	
GOUY	3/11-4/11	—	Coy. took over from 62nd Field Coy. 14th Div. 3 sections in the orders of Lt. Col. 36th-2 Inf. Bde. 1 section at WARLUS under CRE 12th Div. G transport at WARLUS.	
AGNY	5/11	—		
"	6/11 to 30/11	—	Coy. employed as above. 3 sections in the line & highly employed on Dugout Construction - defences of AGNY - Decauville tramways - drying rooms - gas protection to dugouts - various incidental job. 1 section at WARLUS employed in back area - water supply, pumps, huts etc.	

Stenwill Capt. RE.
O.C. 70th Co. RE

30/11

Vol 14

War Diary
70th Field Company R.E.
Vol. 14
Period. 1/12/16 – 31/12/16

Army Form C. 2118.

SECRET

WAR DIARY
INTELLIGENCE SUMMARY
(Erase heading not required.)

70th Field Co. R.E.
12th Div.
December 1916

Place	Date	Hour	Summary of Events and Information	Remarks and references to Appendices
Field	1st–16th	—	3 sections attached to 36th Inf. Bde. for work in Laving Sector south of ARRAS – dugouts, trench tramway, upkeep of trenches, h.g. V.T.M. emplacements, water supply etc. Transport at WARLUS. 1 Section employed under C.R.E. in back area at WARLUS – later supply, hub etc.	
	16th		Company concentrated at GOUY – relieved by 62nd Field Co. – 12th Div. relieved in the line by 14th Div.	
	17th–18th		Company moves from GOUY to LIGNEREUIL.	
	19th–28th		Company moves from LIGNEREUIL to SERICOURT (near FREVENT). Company in rest at SERICOURT – cleaning equipment etc. this began etc. physical training, company drill, squad drill & rifle exercises. Inspection by G.O.C. 12th Div.	
	29th		Company holds four hours from SERICOURT to HAUTEVILLE.	
	30th		Company holds four hours from HAUTEVILLE to GOUVES.	
	31st		Cleaning up & improving billets at GOUVES.	
	30–31st		Employed on dugouts at AGNEZ-LES-DUISANS under C.E. VI Corps.	

H. Greenwell Capt. R.E.
O.C. 70th Co. R.E.
31/12/16

YM/15.

WAR DIARY

70th FIELD COMPANY R.E

D. Senior

1.1.17 to 31.1.17

VOL. 17

SECRET

Army Form C. 2118.

SECRET.

WAR DIARY
or
INTELLIGENCE SUMMARY.
(Erase heading not required.)

Place	Date	Hour	Summary of Events and Information	Remarks and references to Appendices
Gouy	1st 6th 23		Company employed on Burrowing in AGNEZ-LES-DUISANS? three Sections & one Section 1st & Gouves	1st 15:23rd 6 & 8th
	8th 16 31st		Company employed on erecting Nissen Huts & construction of Cookhouses, Latrines. in AGNEZ-LES-DUISANS. One Section employed on Improvement of Listening arrangements for horses in AGNEZ-LES-DUISANS GOUVES & MONTENESCOURT. three Section	
	22nd 24th 25th 31st		Two & half Sections moved to Arras Taking over of work & improvement to Billets 1½ Sections on Construction of Bridges 1 Section on Construction of Observation posts.	
	23 to 31st		½ Section employed on running Rd. Yard at LOUEZ	

R.P. Keelan Capt RE
act/o.e. 70th Fe RE
31-1-17

Vol 16.

SECRET

WAR DIARY

70th FIELD COMPANY R.E.

Period 1/2/17 — 28/2/17

VOLUME 18.

Army Form C. 2118.

WAR DIARY

70th Field Co. R.E.   12th Div.

INTELLIGENCE SUMMARY

February 1917

SECRET

Instructions regarding War Diaries and Intelligence Summaries are contained in F.S. Regs., Part II. and the Staff Manual respectively. Title pages will be prepared in manuscript.

(Erase heading not required.)

Place	Date	Hour	Summary of Events and Information	Remarks and references to Appendices
ARRAS	1st to 15th		Company billeted in ARRAS & employs as follows under CRE 12th Div.	
	26th		No.1 Section - 3 Brigade battle headquarters in ST. SAUVEUR.	
			No.2 Section - fixing up roads & repair hotels in & around ARRAS, & 12th Div. transig. station ARRAS	
			No.3 Section - Artillery observation posts.	
			No.4 Section - 3 Brigade battle headquarters for 15th Div.	
			12th Divl. R.I.?	
			2 Aid Posts in INK STREET	
	1st		12 men employed at Wirl. Yard LOUIEZ	
			Lieut. N.R. Hais joined coy. from base.	

J. Stewart, Major R.E.
28/2/17   O.C. 70th Co. R.E.

Vol 17.

WAR DIARY

10th FIELD COMPANY R.E.

to Peronne

1.3.17 to 31.3.17

VOLUME ~~19~~

SECRET

70th Field Co. R.E.   WAR DIARY   12th Div.

Army Form C. 2118.
SECRET

INTELLIGENCE SUMMARY.   March 1917

Place	Date	Hour	Summary of Events and Information	Remarks and references to Appendices
ARRAS	1st to 31st		Company billeted in ARRAS & employed as follows under CRE 12th Div. No. 1 Section - 3 Bn. battle headquarters in ST SAUVEUR - clearing RUE TRIS ECLISSES & bridging trenches crossing same - Sentry posts in right brigade area. No. 2 Section - 12th Div. dressing station in ARRAS - Inf. rest posts in left area - artillery tracks & bridges over trenches. No. 3 Section - artillery observation posts - strengthening cellars in ARRAS No. 4 Section - 3 Aid posts in Jn.k Street.	

JJ Emmett Maj. R.E.
O.C. 70th Field Co. R.E.

31/3/17

SECRET.

10th
Vol 18.

WAR DIARY

70th FIELD COMPANY. R.E

to June

1st to 30/7

VOLUME 20.

SECRET

Army Form C. 2118.

WAR DIARY APRIL 1917. 12th Div.
or
INTELLIGENCE SUMMARY. 70th Fd Coy R.E.

(Erase heading not required.)

Instructions regarding War Diaries and Intelligence Summaries are contained in F. S. Regs., Part II. and the Staff Manual respectively. Title pages will be prepared in manuscript.

Place	Date	Hour	Summary of Events and Information	Remarks and references to Appendices
Arras	1st to 5th		Work under C.R.E. 12th Div. in preparation for attack – arty bridges, O.P.s, strengthening cellars, communication trenches, and posts etc.	
-"-	6th 7th 8th		In Hotel de Ville cellars during bombardment preparatory to Battle of Arras.	
-"-	9th		Attached to 36th Inf. Bde. for consolidation of Black & Blue Lines – 2 strong points in each line constructed.	
-"-	10th		Attached to 37th Inf. Bde. for consolidation of Orange & Chapel Hills – 2 strong points constructed.	
Feuchy Chapel	11th		Coy. moved to Feuchy Chapel – attached to 36th Inf. Bde. – 2 strong points consolidated near Monchy-le-Preux.	
Rinville	12th		Coy. in rest.	
-"-	13th		Coy. moved to Ronville Caves near Arras.	
Nayelette	14th		B.H. rest in Ronville Caves	
Mondicourt	15th		Coy. moved to Nayelette.	
-"-	16th 17th 18th		Coy. moved to hut camp nr Mondicourt	
-"-	19th 20th 21st		Coy in rest – general clean up & overhaul of equipment. Construction of Prisoners Camp near Souastre under C.E. XVIII Corps	
-"-	22nd		Construction of Prisoners Camp near Halloy under C.E. XVIII Corps.	
Wanquetin	23rd		Coy in rest	
Arras	24th		Coy moved to Wanquetin	
-"-	25th		Coy moved to Arras	
Railway	26th 27th		Coy moved to Railway Triangle near Arras	
Feuchy	30th		Coy attached to 36th Inf. Bde. for consolidation of Orange Hill. Coy moved to Feuchy.	

J.R. Edmund Maj. R.E.
O.C. 70th Fd Coy R.E.
30/4/17

No 19.

Confidential

War Diary
of
70th Field Co. R.E.

from May 1, 1917 to May 31, 1917

Volume 21.

SECRET.

Army Form C. 2118.

MAY 1917

70th Field C.R.E. (12th Division)

WAR DIARY
INTELLIGENCE SUMMARY.
(Erase heading not required)

Instructions regarding War Diaries and Intelligence Summaries are contained in F. S. Regs., Part II. and the Staff Manual respectively. Title pages will be prepared in manuscript.

Place	Date	Hour	Summary of Events and Information	Remarks and references to Appendices
FEUCHY	1st-15th		Coy. employed under 36th & 37th Inf. Bdes. on consolidation of SCABBARD, ELBOW, WRIST, NEW, RIFLE, BAYONET & HARNESS Trenches.	
"	3rd		Attack by 36th Inf. Bde. – 3 strong points constructed	
"	12th		Attack by 37th Inf. Bde. – attack fails – coy. not employed.	
ARRAS	16th		Coy. moves to ARRAS	
GOUVES	17th		Coy. moves to GOUVES – 1 section – NISSEN huts at WAGONLIEU.	
"	18th-23rd		Coy. in rest at GOUVES –	
IVERGNY	24th		Coy. moved to IVERGNY.	
"	25th-31st		Coy. in rest at IVERGNY – general overhaul of equipment & clothing – drill & sports.	

[signature] Major R.E.
O.C. 70th C.R.E.
31/5/17

Vol 20

Confidential

War Diary

of

70th Field Coy R.E.

from June 1, 1917 — to June 30, 1917

Volume 22

Original

SECRET

Army Form C. 2118.

WAR DIARY 70th Field Co. R.E.
INTELLIGENCE SUMMARY. (12th Div.)

(Erase heading not required.)

June 1917.

Place	Date	Hour	Summary of Events and Information	Remarks and references to Appendices
IVERGNY	1st to 16th		Coy in rest at IVERGNY — general overhaul of equipment & clothing — Drill, musketry, field works, sports & concerts.	
GOUVES	17th 18th		Coy moved to GOUVES	
ARRAS	18th		Coy moved to ARRAS	
In the field	19th		Coy moved to OBSERVATION HILL — 12th Div. took over line in front of MONCHY from 3rd Div.	
— " —	20th to 30th		Coy employed under C.R.E. & with 36th & 37th Inf Bde in the line — construction of deep dugouts, reclamation of trenches, demolition of ranging marks, water supply etc.	
	19th		2/Lieut. GILMORE left coy to proceed to England.	

J. Stennvill Maj. R.E.
O.C. 70th Co. R.E.

30/6/17

Vol 21.

Confidential

War Diary

of

70th Field Co. R.E.

from July 1, 1917 to July 31, 1917

VOLUME 23.

Secret

WAR DIARY
INTELLIGENCE SUMMARY
(Erase heading not required.)

Army Form C. 2118.

Place	Date	Hour	Summary of Events and Information	Remarks and references to Appendices
In the Field	1st/6 31st		Coy employed on consolidation of trenches in front of Monchy le Preux - dugouts, wiring - fire stepping - trench digging - provision of Inf. shelters etc 1st 6-8th - under C.R.E. v working with 26th Inf Bde. 9th to 24th - attached to 33rd Inf Bde. 23rd to 9/25 - attached to 37th Inf Bde. attack on Long Trench } both attacks failed v coy not used. attack on Devils Trench } 2/Lieut N. Hinks joined coy.	

J Churchill Major R.E.
O.C. 70th Coy R.E.

Vol 22

Confidential

War Diary
of
70th Field Co. R.E.

From Aug. 1, 1917 to Aug. 31, 1917.

VOLUME 24.

August 1917. 70th Field Co. RE — 12th Division. Secret

WAR DIARY
INTELLIGENCE SUMMARY.

Army Form C. 2118.

Place	Date	Hour	Summary of Events and Information	Remarks and references to Appendices
In the field	1st to 31st	—	Coy working in left brigade area (Monchy subsector) of 12th Division area, in front of Monchy-le-Preux under each of 35th, 36th & 37th Bdes, in turn. Work chiefly wiring, dugouts, trench boarding, revetting & fire-stepping of trenches, etc.	
	9.15		16 o.d. of coy employed in raid on Boche trenches under 37th Bde. — for purpose of blowing up dugouts etc.	

J.S. Stannwell Maj. RE.
O.C. 70th F. Coy RE.

31/8/17

Vol 23

Confidential

War Diary

of

70th Field Co. R.E.

from Sep. 1, 1917 to Sep 30, 1917

VOLUME 25

September 1917. 70th *Field Coy.* WAR DIARY
R.E. INTELLIGENCE SUMMARY.
12th *DIVISION.*

Army Form C. 2118.

Secret

Place	Date	Hour	Summary of Events and Information	Remarks and references to Appendices
In the field	1st to 30th	—	Coy. working in left b.c. area (MONCHY subsector) of 12th Div. area in front of MONCHY-LE-PREUX. under 35 D & 36 D Bns. in turn. Work chiefly wiring & dug-outs, constructing fire-stepping & reinforcing trenches, protected wiring/posts & infantry shelters.	
	10th to 36th		No. 2 section employed under CRE 12th Division on hut & horse-standings in back area.	
	25th to 30th		No. 4 Section ——ditto——	

Stennett Major R.E.
O.C. 70th Co R.E.

3017

WA 24.

Confidential

War Diary

of

70th Field Co. R.E.

October 1, 1917 to October 31, 1917

VOLUME 26.

70th Field Company, R.E.
1st Division

Secret
Army Form C. 2118.

WAR DIARY
-or-
INTELLIGENCE SUMMARY. October 1917. Volume 26
(Erase heading not required)

Place	Date	Hour	Summary of Events and Information	Remarks and references to Appendices
In the Field	1st to 23rd		Two Sections employed with 35th & 36th Inf. Bdes. alternately in the line in front of Moeuvres–V-Prenur on revetting & firestepping trenches, using protecto sentry posts etc. Two Sections employed under CRE 12th Div. erecting heaps & hoarstandings in Bivouac Delsicourt Ronville & Tilloy.	
24th		1 Section accompanies 1st Norfolk Regt. in large raid east of Moeuvres–V-Prenur for purpose of demolishing dugouts.	
24th-25th		Div. relieved in the line by 54th Div. Coy. proceeds to Hautecourt.	
26th		Coy. proceeds to Grands Rullecourt.	
27th		Coy. transport proceeds to Achiet le Petit. Coy. transport proceeds to Heudecourt & dismounted portion of Coy. entrained at Saulty & proceeds to Heudecourt.	
29th to 31st		Coy. employed in erecting Furnac shelters at Heudecourt under III Corps.	

E.D. Pennill Major R.E.
OC 70th Co. R.E.

35th/7

Vol 25

Confidential

War Diary of
10th Field Co. R.E.

From Nov. 1. 1917. to Nov. 29. 1917

VOLUME 27

Confidential

Army Form C. 2118.

WAR DIARY of 70th Field Co. R.E.

INTELLIGENCE SUMMARY. for NOVEMBER 1917

(Erase heading not required.)

Instructions regarding War Diaries and Intelligence
Summaries are contained in F. S. Regs., Part II.
and the Staff Manual respectively. Title pages
will be prepared in manuscript.

Place	Date	Hour	Summary of Events and Information	Remarks and references to Appendices
In the field	12/11 13/11 14/11 15/11		Coy at Heudecourt working under CRE 12th Div. (III Corps) erecting bivouac shelters in Heudecourt & at Revelon Farm.	
	15/11 16/11 19/11		Coy moves to Cross Roads Camp (1 mile east of Heudecourt). erecting bivouac shelters in Guyencourt & Sorel court & making tuf tracks & tank crossings in Divl. area.	
	20/11		Coy moved to Villers Ghislain - Battle for Cambrai commenced - Coy with 100 attached Inf. working under 36th Inf. Bde	
	21/11 25/11 26/11 27/11		Coy employed under 36th Inf. Bde in consolidation of captured position (1 Sect under CRE roads & coads). Coy moved to Gonnelieu.	

J S Stanwell Major R.E.
O.C. 70 Co. R.E.

30/11/17

WD 26

Confidential

War Diary of 7O"Fd Co.R.E.

from Dec.1 1917 To Dec.31 1917.

VOLUME 28

Confidential

WAR DIARY of 70th Field Coy. R.E.
INTELLIGENCE SUMMARY. for December 1917

Army Form C. 2118.

(Erase heading not required.)

Place	Date	Hour	Summary of Events and Information	Remarks and references to Appendices
	Dec 3rd		Coy returned to HEUDICOURT.	
	" 4th		Coy moved to CATIGNY	
	" 5th		Coy moved to MEAULTE & stays there till 8th.	
	" 8th		Coy entrains at DERNANCOURT for AIRE, & from there marches to BLOMINGHAM.	
			Coy resting, training & re-equipping with OSE 23rd	
	Dec 23rd		Coy marches to FOREST	
	Dec 26th		Coy marches to LA MOTTE BAUDET.	
	Dec 29th		Coy moves to ARMENTIERES, working on Corps Defences until end of month.	
	Nov 30th		Coy (LESS 500x M.E.) of GONNELIEU. During enemy surprise attack, Coy rendered assistance in holding up attack holding a Trench (GIN AVENUE) North of GONNELIEU.	
	Dec 1st & 2nd		Coy at Tank H.Q. in VILLERS PLOUICH, employed in carrying bombs & ammunition	

R. Lindgren Capt R.E.
O.C./OC. 70 Fd Co R.E.

12th DIVISIONAL ENGINEERS

70th FIELD COMPANY R.E.

JANUARY 1918

WD 27

Confidential

War Diary of 70ᵗʰ Fd. Co. R.E.

from Jan 1, 1918 to Jan 31, 1918

VOLUME 29.

Confidential

WAR DIARY
INTELLIGENCE SUMMARY

No. 170 Field Coy R.E.   for January 1918

Army Form C. 2118.

Place	Date	Hour	Summary of Events and Information	Remarks and references to Appendices
ARMEN-TIERES	1st to 15th		Coy employed under CE XV Corps on Corps Defences - M.G. shelters, wiring & overhauling trenches.	
	16th		Coy moved to NOUVEAU MONDE - transport to BAC ST. MAUR.	
NOUVEAU MONDE	17th to 31st		Coy employed under CRE 12th Div. on FLEURBAIX defences. - M.G. cupolas, wiring, & strong points. (120 O.R. & 3 Offs. from 36th Inf. Bde. attached to Coy. during whole of this period.)	

S. Purnell Major R.E.
OC 170th Coy R.E.

30/1/18

12th DIVISIONAL ENGINEERS

70th FIELD COMPANY R.E.

FEBRUARY 1918

Vol 28.

Confidential

War Diary of 70th Fd. Coy. R.E.

from Feb. 1, 1918 to Feb 28, 1918.

VOLUME 30

Confidential

70th Field Coy R.E. WAR DIARY or INTELLIGENCE SUMMARY

Army Form C. 2118.

February 1918.

Place	Date	Hour	Summary of Events and Information	Remarks and references to Appendices
	1st to 28th	—	Coy employed under CRE 12th Divn. on Theisbow defences & in Divl. Battle Zone - concrete M.G. emplts, wiring strong points. (1 officer & 90 OR (average) from 36th Inf Bde attached to coy during the whole of the period).	
	2nd	—	Coy moved from NOUVEAU MONDE to BAC ST. MAUR.	

J. Rennell Huey, RE.
O.C. 70 Coy R.E.

28/2/18

12th Divisional Engineers.

WAR DIARY

70th FIELD COMPANY R. E.

MARCH 1918

Vol 29

Confidential

War Diary of 10th Ja. Coy R.E.

from March 1st 1918 to March 31st 1918.

VOLUME 31.

70th F. Co. R.E.

Confidential
Army Form C. 2118.

WAR DIARY
~~INTELLIGENCE~~ SUMMARY
March, 1918.

(Erase heading not required.)

Instructions regarding War Diaries and Intelligence Summaries are contained in F. S. Regs., Part II. and the Staff Manual respectively. Title pages will be prepared in manuscript.

Place	Date	Hour	Summary of Events and Information	Remarks and references to Appendices
BAC ST MAUR	1st 16th 19th		Coy. employed under CRE, 12th Div: — on battle zone in vicinity of FLEURBAIX — m.g. emplts. trenches, wiring etc.	
—"—	3rd		Lieut: C.R.B. Duke left coy. on appointment to Adjt. CRE. 51st Div.	
	20th		Coy. moved as follows — Nos. 1 & 3 Sech. & HQrs. to CROIX DU BAC — No. 2 Section to VERQUINGHEM — No. 4 & transport to near ESTAIRES.	
	21st 22nd 23rd		Coy. employed under C.E. XV Corps on LYS RIVER line — trenches, wiring	
	23rd		Transport moves to LE SART & No. 2 Section to CROIX DU BAC	
	24th		Transport by road & Coy by bus to OBLINGHEM (near BETHUNE) then marches to FOUQUIERES & entrances for BOUZAINCOURT	
	25th		Transport to CAMBLIGNEUL — Coy. resting & standing to in near BOUZAINCOURT	
	26th		Transport to LUCHEUX — Coy. standing to near BOUZAINCOURT & blowing up bridges over RIVER ANCRE	
	27th		Transport to FORCEVILLE — Coy. digging trenches near BOUZAINCOURT	
	28th		Coy. moves to HEDAUVILLE — —"—	
	29th		Coy. moves to WARLOY — —"—	
	30th		Transport moves to CONTAY — Coy. in rest at WARLOY	
	31st		—"— —"—	

W.B.R.L.
Major R.E.
O.C. 70th Co. R.E.

31/3/18

12th Div.

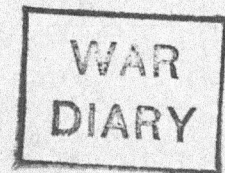

70th FIELD COMPANY, R.E.

APRIL

1918

M 30

Confidential

War Diary of 70th In. Co. R.E.

From 1st April 1918. to 30th April 1918.

Volume 32

Confidential
Army Form C. 2118.

170th Co. Coy R.E.

WAR DIARY for April 1918.

INTELLIGENCE SUMMARY
(Erase heading not required.)

Instructions regarding War Diaries and Intelligence Summaries are contained in F. S. Regs., Part II. and the Staff Manual respectively. Title pages will be prepared in manuscript.

Place	Date	Hour	Summary of Events and Information	Remarks and references to Appendices
WARLOY	1st–2nd		Coy employed under I Corps on Army Line trenches near WARLOY.	
	2nd		Coy moved to SENLIS - Transport to WARLOY. - 12th Div. into the line near ALBERT.	
SENLIS	3rd–4th		Support line trenches & wiring of same near ALBERT.	
	5th		Coy standing to in Corps line - German attack repulsed.	
	6th		Coy moved to 500x north west of SENLIS - wiring Corps line.	
	7th–10th		wiring Corps line near BOUZAINCOURT.	
	11th		Coy moved to WARLOY.	
WARLOY	12th–23rd		Coy employed under I Corps on Army Line near WARLOY & Corps line near HENENCOURT including 4 days in rest - baths clean up etc.	
	24th		Coy moves to ACHEUX - 12th Div. into the line near BEAUMONT-HAMEL.	
ACHEUX	25th–30th		Coy employed under CRE on 2nd system near MAILLY-MAILLET - 1 Sect. living at MAILLY-MAILLET & working in the line under 35th Bde.	

30/4/18

J. Stanwell Maj. R.E.
O.C. 170th Co. R.E.

12th DIVISIONAL ENGINEERS

70th FIELD COMPANY R.E.

MAY   1918

Vol 33

Confidential

War Diary of 70th Field Coy R.E.

From 1st May 1918 to 31st May 1918

Volume 33.

Army Form C. 2118.
Confidential

70th Field Co. R.E. WAR DIARY for May 1918
INTELLIGENCE SUMMARY.
(Erase heading not required.)

Instructions regarding War Diaries and Intelligence Summaries are contained in F. S. Regs., Part II. and the Staff Manual respectively. Title pages will be prepared in manuscript.

Place	Date	Hour	Summary of Events and Information	Remarks and references to Appendices
Arras ACHEUX	1st – 2nd		12th Div. in the line in front of AUCHONVILLERS – 1 sect. attached to 85th Inf. Bde. for work in the line – dugouts, batt's + coy H.Q. making trenchboards, duckboards etc – gas proofing dugouts etc	
	4th – 13th – 15th – 17th – 20th		3 sects. working under CRE. 12th Div on 2nd system between MAILLY-MAILLET and AUCHONVILLERS – trench training emergency tracks etc	
	26th		Transport horses from ACHEUX to LOUVENCOURT Wood Coy moves from ACHEUX to Louvencourt Wood	
	27-28		Lt. Ellem 77th Div. U.S. Army attached for instruction. Coy Transport moves to BEAUQUESNE – 12th Div. Can all fit in	
	29.31		Rest + clean up. Coy training – physical exercises, fieldworks, squad drill rifle exercises etc preliminary musketry	
	29th		No. 2 Sect + 1 Platoon 7th Royal Sussex moves to LEALVILLERS for work on adv. Div. H.Q. Ora.	
	31st –		Inspection of transport by G.O.C. Div.	

J. Stewart Major RE
OC 70 Co RE
31/5/18

12th DIVISIONAL ENGINEERS

70th FIELD COMPANY R.E.

JUNE 1918

No 32

Confidential

War Diary of 4th Field Bty CFA

From June 1st 1918 to June 30th 1918

Volume 3rd

70 jcbc R.E.

WAR DIARY for JUNE, 1918.

Army Form C. 2118.
Confidential

INTELLIGENCE SUMMARY.

Place	Date	Hour	Summary of Events and Information	Remarks and references to Appendices
BEAUQ-UESNE	1st - 15		Coy. in rest at BEAUQUESNE - training & refitting - musketry, field works instruction, open order drill, close order drill etc.	
	16th			
	16th-3		One section meeting Advance Div¹ H⁰ Qrs near LEALVILLERS - reformed coy on 5th formed	
	17th 7		Inspection of 36th Bde. group by Corps Commander.	
	17th		Ordered Lt. from 36th V Bde. rejoined their battalion	
	18th-1 30		12th Div. relieves 35th Div. in the line near BOUZINCOURT - completes 205th field Co. - & hopes to use SENLIS.	
			Coy. employed in right Bde. area with 36th Inf. Bde. R.E. - winning, dugouts, new reserve line, CT's etc.	

J Brunwell Maj R.E.
29/6/18 O.C. 70 Coy R.E.

12th DIVISIONAL ENGINEERS

70th FIELD COMPANY R.E.

JULY 1918

WD 33.

Confidential

War Diary of 70th Fd Coy R.E.

from July 1. 1918 to July 31, 1918.

VOLUME 35.

July 31, 1918.   Confidential

Army Form C. 2118.

WAR DIARY of 170th Fld C.R.E.
or
INTELLIGENCE SUMMARY.
(Erase heading not required.)

Instructions regarding War Diaries and Intelligence Summaries are contained in F. S. Regs., Part II. and the Staff Manual respectively. Title pages will be prepared in manuscript.

Place	Date	Hour	Summary of Events and Information	Remarks and references to Appendices
Near Senlis	1st		Coy employed in right Sr. area BOUZINCOURT sector – 2 sects under B.C.	
-"-	9th		2 sects under C.R.E. – wiring + digging reserve line, deep dugouts etc.	
-"-	5th		Lt. Col. Bovet CRE killed – Maj. Gemmell takes 5th – 12th	
-"-	10th		12th Div. relieved in the line by 17th Div. – Coy moved to TOUTENCOURT WOOD	
TOUTENCOURT	11th		Coy in rest – general clean up + overhaul of equipment transport etc	
-"-	12th			
-"-	13th		Transport moved to RENANCOURT (near AMIENS)	
-"-	14th		Coy entrained at PUCHEVILLERS – detrained at CONTRE marched to BLANGY 15015-POIX – Transport rejoined Coy at BLANGY.	
	15th		Coy + transport moved to FLERS-SUR-NOYE – now in IX Corps	
FLERS	16th		Coy in rest at FLERS – Coy training physical training bayonet	
-"-	27th		fighting, open + close order drill, field works instruction, sports etc	
-"-	30th		Coy moved to VIGNACOURT – transport by road – remainder by Rail via LOEUILLY.	
VIGNACOURT	31st		General clean up of transport etc - now in III Corps.	

J. Gemmell Maj. R.E.
O.C. 170th Coy R.E.

31/7/18

12th Divisional Engineers

70th FIELD COMPANY,

ROYAL ENGINEERS,

A U G U S T, 1 9 1 8.

Vol 34.

Confidential

War Diary of 46th Field Company R.E.

August 1st 1918 to August 31st 1918.

Volume 36.

Confidential

Army Form C. 2118.

WAR DIARY of 70th Field Coy R.E.

INTELLIGENCE SUMMARY.

August 1918.

(Erase heading not required.)

Instructions regarding War Diaries and Intelligence Summaries are contained in F. S. Regs., Part II. and the Staff Manual respectively. Title pages will be prepared in manuscript.

Place	Date	Hour	Summary of Events and Information	Remarks and references to Appendices
VIGNACOURT	1st	—	Coy in rest.	
	2nd	—	Coy moved to near RIBEMONT - transport to BAISIEUX - 12th Div. relieved 58th Div.	
RIBEMONT	3rd-7th	—	In the line. 70th Co. relieves 504th Cy.	
"	8th	—	1/2 Co. under CRE 1/2 Co. under 35th Bde - breastworks bridges & Bath Arts.	
"	9th	—	12th Div. attack - coy consolidating 35th Bde front.	
"	10th	—	Battle continues - MORLANCOURT captured - work on roads.	
"	21st	—	1/2 Co. under CRE 1/2 Co. under 35th. Then 37th. Then 36th Bdes. - strong points, wiring reserve line, Bde & Batt. HQs. Dns. etc.	
"	20th	—	Transport moved to HERICOURT - 2 Recn. to VILLE-SUR-ANCRE	
"	22nd	—	12th Div attack - MEAULTE captured - 1/2 Co. under CRE on tracks 1/2 Co. consolidating 35th Bde front. 2 sect. moved to VILLE-SUR-ANCRE	
VILLE	23-24	—	Reserve line & well in MEAULTE	
	25	—	Coy & transport moved to near BECORDEL - water supplies MEAULTE & FRICOURT	
BECORDEL	26-28	—	1 sect. attached to 36th Bde from 25th-K31st for operations. Water Supplies MEAULTE & MAMETZ	
	29	—	Coy transport moved to MAMETZ - repairing roads.	
MAMETZ	30-31st	—	Water supplies MAMETZ & MONTAUBAN MAMETZ - 47th Div. went through 12th Div.	

31/8/18

Stokenwill Major R.E.
O.C. 70th Co. R.E.

12th DIVISIONAL ENGINEERS

70th FIELD COMPANY R.E.

SEPTEMBER 1918

№ 35

Confidential

War Diary of 1st Field Company R.E.

September 1st 1918 to September 30th 1918

Volume 34

Confidential   September 1918   7th Field Company. R.E.

Army Form C. 2118.

WAR DIARY
INTELLIGENCE SUMMARY.
(Erase heading not required.)

Place	Date	Hour	Summary of Events and Information	Remarks and references to Appendices
MAMETZ	1/9/18		Coy moved to MAMETZ. working on forward water Supply. No 4 Section attached to 36th Inf Brig Hd.	
	4/9/18		At work during September with Lt Thirwell, 2 Lts Parr & Butchmunson on M.E. Lt the latter RE/Ammunition on M.E. Major Guined M.C., R.E. handed over command of Coy to Major Keelan on departure to take up new appointment with 24 Base Park Coy R.E.	
COMBLES	4/9/18		Coy moved to COMBLES. working on forward water supply & filtering of pumps & engines in COMBLES	
	5/9/18		Took over work from 80 Coy R.E. 18 Div. Lt GUTHRIE RE. given from 16 Field Coy for duty as 2nd in command.	
MANANCOURT	6/9/18		Coy moves to Manancourt. Working on forward water supply. No 4 Section rejoins Coy on 10th. Building of Div. H.Q. near NURLU.	
LIERAMONT	17/9/18		Coy moves to LIERAMONT. Lying up to 6 am attached to 36th Inf Brigade for operations. Coy working on water supply in GUYENCOURT & SAULCOURT & development of water supply in NURLU & LIERAMONT. also Reconnaissance of water supply in EPEHY. by which on NURLU Baths and even emerald tanks. Clearing minefield on Div. Front.	
	24/9/18		Took over work with 37th Inf Bde from 97 Field Coy handing over 36th Inf Bde work to same company	
	28/9/18		Coy new work with 36" Inf Bde 87"-	
			B.O.R. attached to 36th Inf Bde for operation Company at disposal of C.E. III corps for purpose of making bridge over ESCAUT RIVER at near VENDHUILE	
	29/9/18		Bridge prepared, company standing by	

B.R.Keelan Major R.E.
o.c. 7th F.C. R.E.

12th DIVISIONAL ENGINEERS

70th FIELD COMPANY R.E.

OCTOBER 1918

Confidential

War Diary of 70th Field Co RE

Oct 1. 1918 to Oct 31 1918

VOLUME 38

Confidential

WAR DIARY of 70th F.R.E.

October 1918.

Army Form C. 2118.

INTELLIGENCE SUMMARY.

Place	Date	Hour	Summary of Events and Information	Remarks and references to Appendices
LIERMONT	1st		Coy marched from LIERMONT to PERRONNE.	
MERIGNOLLS	2nd	5 A.M.	Coy entrained & detrained at ACQ.	
CHATEAU DE LA HAIE	3rd		Coy. moved to CHATEAU DE LA HAIE.	
VIMY	4th 5th		3 Sections moved to VIMY and took over work in the line from 83rd F.E. 20th Div. employed on water supply and stores at Div HQ. Transport of one Section to NEUVILLE St. VAAST.	
	7th		Transport moved to NEUVILLE St VAAST.	
	11th		Coy with Transport moved to SALLAUMINES.	
SALLAUMINES	12		Maj Keelan returned from leave & took over command from Capt Guthrie. 1 Sect attached 36th Bde	
"	13		Capt Guthrie went on leave & Coy moved to BILLY MONTIGNY working on Roads, water supply & Rwltn	
"	14		Pontoon Bridge on Canal HAUTE DEULE on 16th F.E. Transport Tactile Bridge on canal HAUTE DEULE	
DOURGES	17/18th		Coy moved to DOURGES. 1 Bn. 100ft Span Hora Transport Bridge	
COURTICHES	19th		Coy moved to COURTICHES. Built a 20 Ton bridge to replace culvert demolished by enemy	
LANDAS	21st		Coy moved to LANDAS. employed on sundry crates & making plank Roads & construction of Bridges	
			to replace culverts. Section attached to Brigade repairing roads	
LECELLES	24th		Coy moved to LECELLES. Employed on Roads &c. 1 Section attached to 36th Brigade	
			Coy employed on Roads. Crater Demolition; 6 ton Bridge, 10 & 15ft Spans built over Rvr. SCARPE	
	28th		wt. 120# PLANK Road to each approach. Heavy Turn in Bridge.	
			Section attached to Brigade wt. 15 th(?) wt 15 built SE goat Bridges over River Decoures & River SCARPE.	
RUE DE ROBURT	29th		Coy moved to RUE DE ROBURT. Co went to re-equip & re-outfit Div in nothing further took, Section attached	
	30th 31st		to Brigades repairing Co.	
			Coy training &c.	

R Keelan
Maj R.E.
O.C. 70th F.C. R.E.

12th DIVISIONAL ENGINEERS

70th FIELD COMPNAY R. E.

NOVEMBER 1918

Confidential   Vol 37

War Diary of 76th Field C.R.E.

Nov. 1 1918 to Nov 30 1918

VOLUME 39.

Confidential

WAR DIARY of "70" Field Co. R.E. Army Form C. 2118.

INTELLIGENCE SUMMARY.
(Erase heading not required.)

for NOVEMBER, 1918.

Instructions regarding War Diaries and Intelligence Summaries are contained in F. S. Regs., Part II. and the Staff Manual respectively. Title pages will be prepared in manuscript.

Place	Date	Hour	Summary of Events and Information	Remarks and references to Appendices
ROSULT	1st to 7th		Coy in rest area Training	
ODOMEZ	8th		Coy moves to ODOMEZ. worked on construction of steam waggon Track Bridge on Jard Canal, also on construction of plank Road	
"	11th		Armistice signed. Coy carries on on usual works on Roads & filling Craters	
STAMBRUGES	19th to 25th		Coy moves to STAMBRUGES. worked on construction of Bridge at this place. also constructs 19Ton Bridge 90 ft long at GRANDGLISES and carries on repairs to roads, remaking of turn in road at STAMBRUGES.	
ST AMAND	25th		Coy moves to St AMAND	
ANICHE	26th	5.30	Coy moves to ANICHE. working on construction of Workshops for electrical purposes, & general development of electrical scheme	

R Phelan
Major RE
OC 70 FD. CE.

12th DIVISIONAL ENGINEERS

70th FIELD COMPANY R.E.

DECEMBER 1918

U.D. 38

Confidential

War Diary of 10th Field Co. R.E.

Dec. 1. 1918. to Dec. 31. 1918.

Volume 40

Confidential

Army Form C. 2118.

WAR DIARY of 70 "Field" R.E.
or
INTELLIGENCE SUMMARY. for December 1918.

(Erase heading not required.)

Instructions regarding War Diaries and Intelligence Summaries are contained in F. S. Regs., Part II. and the Staff Manual respectively. Title pages will be prepared in manuscript.

Place	Date	Hour	Summary of Events and Information	Remarks and references to Appendices
ANICHE	1-12-18 to 31-12-18		Billetted at Aniche. Educational Scheme. Work on Dowchingler Camp SOMAINE. Work in Brigade area on Recreation Room. Cement Walls, & Bath Houses. Repairs to Civilian property. Development of Electric Light installation. Inspection by G.O.C. Division 23-12-18.	

Signature
Major R.E.
O.C. 70 F.C.R.E.

WD 39
12/

Confidential

War Diary of

10th Field Co. Royal Engineers

from Jan 1 1919 to Jan 31 1919

VOLUME 41

Confidential

WAR DIARY of 70th Field Co. R.E.
or
INTELLIGENCE SUMMARY.   for January 1919.

Army Form C. 2118.

(Erase heading not required.)

Place	Date	Hour	Summary of Events and Information	Remarks and references to Appendices
ANICHE	1.1.19 – 31.1.19		Billeted at ANICHE. Work on demobilization camps SOMAIN and hand FENAIN & ERRE. Repairs to civilian property. Development of Electric Light continues. Demobilization commenced on 11-12-18	

E.P. Irvine Capt. RE
Off OC. 70 Field Coy RE.

WO 40

Confidential

War Diary of
7th Field Coy. Royal Engineers

from Feb. 1st 1919 to Feb 28th 1919

Volume 42.

Confidential

Army Form C. 2118.

Instructions regarding War Diaries and Intelligence Summaries are contained in F.S. Regs., Part II. and the Staff Manual respectively. Title pages will be prepared in manuscript.

WAR DIARY
or
INTELLIGENCE SUMMARY.
(Erase heading not required.)

4th Field Coy. R.E.

Place	Date	Hour	Summary of Events and Information	Remarks and references to Appendices
ANICHE	17th to 28th Feb		Coy employed on construction of demolished Canal Somain. R&S repairs in neighbouring area. Construction of Ramps at ANICHE Station. Strength of Coy practically down to O.Gor. It Young left for Egypt on 17th. 20 N.S. drawings in Young's	

B.R. Sykes
Major O.C. 4th Field Coy.

WO 41.

Confidential

War Diary of "70" Field Company R.E.

from Mar 1/99 to Mar 31/99

VOLUME 43

Confidential

War Diary of 70th Field Coy R.E.

Army Form C. 2118.

WAR DIARY
INTELLIGENCE SUMMARY.
(Erase heading not required.)

Place	Date	Hour	Summary of Events and Information	Remarks and references to Appendices
ANICHE	1st March to 31st March		Company employed on construction of Ramps at ANICHE & SOMAIN. 1 Lt Barnett proceeded to 62 Div on 2nd for leave of Occupation	

E.G. Ritchie
Capt R.E.
a/O.C. 70th Field Coy R.E.

WD 44

Confidential

War Diary of 76th Field Co. R.E.

from April 1. 1919 to April 30. 1919

VOLUME 44

Confidential

WAR DIARY of 70th Field Co R.E.

INTELLIGENCE SUMMARY.

Army Form C. 2118.

(Erase heading not required.)

Place	Date	Hour	Summary of Events and Information	Remarks and references to Appendices
ANICHE	April 1st to 30th 1919		Company employed on various odd jobs in vicinity.	
			ANICHE.	
			Capt. E.G. GUTHRIE M.C. R.E. appointed Third Col: R.E. 5/4/19 and proceeds to	
			Lt. W.H. HOWELL proceeds on leave 19.4.19. VALENCIENNES duty	
			(Special).	
			Major R.E. KEERAN M.C. R.E. demobilizes 20.4.19.	
			Capt: A.E. DALGAS M.C. R.E. took on temporary Command 20/4/19.	
			" A.E. " " demobilizes 21/4/19 and proceeds	
			Major V. AM. ROBERTSON. M.C. R.E, took on temporary command 21/4/19.	
			R. an Roberts Major R.E. 70th Field Coy R.E.	
			A.f.o.c. 70th	

27/8

9746.3

12

Confidential

War Diary of 70th Field Co RE.

from May 1 1919 to May 16 1919

Volume 45

Confidential

Army Form C. 2118.

WAR DIARY of 70th Fd. Coy. RE
INTELLIGENCE SUMMARY. May 1919.

(Erase heading not required.)

Instructions regarding War Diaries and Intelligence Summaries are contained in F. S. Regs., Part II. and the Staff Manual respectively. Title pages will be prepared in manuscript.

Place	Date	Hour	Summary of Events and Information	Remarks and references to Appendices
ANICHE	May 1 - May 6		Company employed on preparation for embarkation	
	May 7		Company left ANICHE, entraining at SOMAIN, for DUNKIRK.	
	May 10		Company embarked from DUNKIRK for SOUTHAMPTON.	
			End of War Diary of 70th Fd. C. R.E.	

M Mitchell Major, R.E.
O.C. 70th Fd. Coy. R.E.

www.ingramcontent.com/pod-product-compliance
Lightning Source LLC
Chambersburg PA
CBHW080857230426
43663CB00013B/2568